FROM HOLY HELL TO HALLELUJAH AGAIN!

FROM HOLY HELL
TO HALLELUJAH AGAIN!
SURVIVING THE CONSUMING FLAMES
OF CONGREGATIONAL CONFLICT

EVERTON A. ENNIS, D.MIN.

DENVER, COLORADO

Outskirts Press, Inc.
http://www.outskirtspress.com

ISBN: 978-1-4787-5781-8

Library of Congress Control Number: 2015921412

Outskirts Press and the "OP" logo are trademarks belonging to Outskirts Press, Inc.

PRINTED IN THE UNITED STATES OF AMERICA

# Preface

I did not expect the fury of anger and the depth of conflict I encountered within three weeks of my installation as the new pastor. Worse yet, I was totally unprepared to manage it. Neither my undergraduate ministerial training nor my Master of Divinity degree from our seminary had prepared me for anything like what I had walked into. What was envisioned as an exciting, productive and fulfilling ministry had suddenly been transformed into my worst nightmare. It was as if I had walked into the middle of a holy hell!

No one told me that church folks could be so angry, so callous, so vitriolic, and so evil! I had been in the church for fifteen years prior to assuming my new role as a pastor. I had lived in a total of three countries, been a member of several congregations, and had seen some terrible church fights between members, and between members and pastors. Still, I was unprepared for this. It was a new experience. This was different. Now I was the pastor, the one toward whom the frustrations of yesteryear and today, plus the fears concerning tomorrow, were now directed.

Somewhere, somehow, in all the years of academic training I had received to prepare me to lead churches, someone forgot to tell me about the less joyful side of pastoral ministry – when the pastor is the target of someone's wrath, when an angry saint puts a crosshair on his forehead. I had seen it happen to some of my former pastors, but now, it had become my reality. Now I knew what they must have felt like, as they were mercilessly criticized, slandered, and in the timeless words of Jesus, "reviled" and "persecuted". Yes, those words came to have special significance for me. I have had many reflections of Jesus saying, "for so persecuted they the prophets who were before you."

My denominational leaders seemed to have been clueless about what was going on in this church before sending me there. It must have been so, since no one bothered to alert me in any way prior to my arrival or installation. To make matters worse, when the ferocious flames of congregational conflict began to intensify, I got the feeling that the concern from some denominational leaders was "Now, what did he go there and do wrong?" Needless to say, the problems in the church did not start upon or because of my arrival!

This is one aspect of conflict that I will address in this book – congregational dysfunction due to unending conflict.

After much prayer, trial and error, sweat, and tears, the good Lord somehow helped me to figure out how to navigate the obstacle course of congregational conflict in that particular church, and by His grace, I eventually overcame. The church eventually changed from a state of holy hell and became one of the more pleasant pastoral experiences I've had. It was hallelujah again! Through it all, I not only learned to trust in Jesus, but I also learned many important lessons and principles in conflict ministry. It wasn't long afterward that some of my colleagues started inviting me to speak to their congregations about conflict. Someone had been watching to see how I would fare!

Later on, as a result of a most painful season in my pastoral ministry and personal life, I was led to pursue a specialization in congregational conflict resolution training for my doctor of ministry degree. This book is partially the result of the research process for my doctorate, as well as the project dissertation, and my years of experience dealing with and teaching in the area of congregational conflict ministry. You might be wondering why I refer to what I do as conflict ministry. This will become clear to you as you read these pages. You will see how God allowed me to experience several phases of serious professional and personal conflict, just so He could prepare me to write this book.

I will be very transparent in this book. It is the only way that I know to teach and share what experience and research have taught me. The illustrations I will share are all real events that actually happened in my pastoral ministry. It is not my goal or desire to embarrass anyone, thus I have not used the real names of individuals. I have not used the real names of churches or revealed their locations. Any personal identifier used is purely coincidental to any actual person, and does not correspond to anyone I have pastored up until the date of this writing.

You are reading this book because you are either going through a season of conflict in your pastorate; or you are a member of a church who is involved in or witnessing major conflict in your congregation; or you are a denominational leader who desires to broaden your understanding of congregational conflict; or you have been assigned this material as part of the required reading for your ministerial training.

Whatever your motivation, this book will challenge you to view conflict from perspectives that you can both relate to, or have never considered before. I wish you happy reading and God's richest blessings in your quest to be a sharper tool in His hand for a transformed church... from Holy Hell to Hallelujah Again!

Table of Contents

Part Four
Healing the Wounds: Another Look at Repentance, Forgiveness & Reconciliation

Part Five
Conflict Ministry Awareness & Training for Ministerial Students, Pastors, and Denominational Leaders

Acknowledgements

First, to my wife Ingrid, who prayed fervently and encouraged me daily throughout the arduous journey of completing my doctor of ministry project dissertation, from which this book is derived. As a pastor's spouse, she has witnessed and experienced much of the suffering brought on by congregational conflict at various times throughout my ministry. Second, to my mother Delores Beswick-Ennis, who instilled in me the desire for knowledge at an early age, and encouraged me throughout my adult life up until the realization of this dream to never stop learning or reaching for my goals. She instilled a thirst for learning in me that has blessed my life. My father Bartholomew Ennis demonstrated to his children, of which I am the first of six, how to work hard. Though I did not intend it, I also learned from his example how to be a work-a-holic, a trait that I continue in my struggles to overcome.

I probably would not have achieved the goal of my first book without the consistent moral and practical support of Dr. Lawrence Hamilton, General Vice President of South Atlantic Conference of Seventh-day Adventists, and Dr. James J. North, my adviser and committee chair throughout my doctor of ministry degree journey at Andrews University. These two men showered me with amazing x ✝

grace, and exemplified endurance in their roles as encouragers and motivators.

This book is a reality because each of these individuals and so many others believed in me, and never wavered in their ardent support of me and my endeavors to produce a work that would bless the Church of the Living God. My gratitude to God for saving me, placing me in the ministry, and placing key people in my life to help bring out what God has put in me, is what fuels my passion to see churches transition From Holy Hell to Hallelujah Again!

Part One

From War in Heaven to Conflict in the Church

CHAPTER 1

The Devil Did What?

It was one of those terrible times very early in my ministry. My mind raced, and my heart pounded heavily against my chest as I drove the forty miles from home to the church. It was a cold January evening. I had left my bride of one year alone at home to make this journey. It was a terrifying drive. "Butterflies" fluttered around in my stomach. My tummy groaned loudly, because although very hungry, I could not eat before leaving home. The "butterflies" would have nothing to do with the delectable meal my wife had prepared.

The occasion was a meeting with the entire membership of the church I pastored at that time. The meeting was not called by me, but by the elders, at least some of them, that is. The way it was represented to me was that "the people" wanted to have a meeting with me to address the state of uneasiness in the church, due to my leadership style and the direction I was taking the church in.

During the meeting, the primary antagonist, an elder who had verbally abused me on several occasions in both church board and church business meetings, took the lead in publicly laying charge after charge against me. Basically, according to him, I was a bad guy, an even poorer leader, and the cause of all the problems in the church! I was devastated. Surely, if I was that bad, and all "the people" came out to tell me so, then this pastoral ministry wasn't looking so promising after all.

I was a rookie pastor, still wet behind the ears, an un-ordained intern. It wasn't long into the meeting before I realized I'd walked right into the middle of a well laid trap. I learned an important lesson that night that has guided me ever since, and from which you, dear reader, will benefit as you read this book.

Here's what I discovered that night about how devious some church folk and how damaging the undersides of pastoral ministry can be to a pastor. During the meeting, a dear sister openly raised the following concerns, "Pastor, why were we asked to come out here on this cold night to deal with these matters that the pastor and the elders should resolve between yourselves? Why are we here... why were we told to come to this meeting? This meeting does not feel right!" Several other members began to also share their similar concerns about the nature and purpose of the meeting. Angry dissent ensued when I replied that "the elders told me that you, 'the people' asked for this meeting. I'm here tonight because I was told that you wanted to express your concerns about my leadership of the church."

That was the moment when I realized that "the people" had not called for the meeting... that the elders who told me about the people's "request", had manipulated me and misused the name of "the people" to call this meeting for their own political purposes... to "expose" and dishonor me before the members. These elders had told me that the people wanted to have a town hall meeting as soon as possible to address "their" concerns about me. Since the request came from "the people", I agreed to meet. Now, it was clear to me that at least some of "the people" didn't know why they were at the meeting. As it turned out, the elders were the ones who called them and told them there would be a meeting! How did that happen?

After securing my consent to have the meeting and confirming my attendance, the elders then telephoned the members, telling them that I was calling for a town hall so that "the people" could air their grouses about me and my leadership! However, when the members saw the elders leveling charge after charge against me in that public forum, several of them, led by the sister mentioned above, began to express their discomfort with the nature and tone of the meeting.

That encounter was one of the most professionally important and emotionally expensive lessons that I learned during the early years of my ministry. My early ministry quickly became an instructive journey in the art of congregational conflict resolution, learned in the "School of Hard Knocks" about how to navigate the often treacherous experiences of pastoral ministry. This book will draw upon my many experiences and the lessons I have learned along the way. I will share with you key strategies in preventing and surviving some of the more damaging pitfalls in congregational conflict.

Why is it that there is so much conflict in churches? If the church is supposed to be a place of peace, harmony, and Christian love, how then, can so much evil behavior and un-Christlike manners be found among God's people? Why do so many Christians seem to know so little about how to prevent or properly resolve conflict, whether at home, at work, or when we congregate on the weekends as the church? Where did conflict come from anyway? These questions provide the opportunity for me to introduce the Great Controversy motif found in Scripture, as a foundation for understanding interpersonal and corporate conflict.

Conflict is portrayed throughout Scripture in various ways. These include inter-personal conflict (Saul and David, or Paul and

Barnabas), international conflict (Israel and their enemies), and the cosmic conflict (Great Controversy) between God and Satan. Conflict is represented as a breakdown in love and harmony or as an intense difference of opinion, resulting in strife or separation in a relationship. There are several biblical words that depict conflict. For example, strife, from the Hebrew ryb (בִּיר), which means dispute in Genesis 13:7; contention, from the Hebrew myrbh (הַ,בִּירְ,מֹ), which indicates a quarrel in Genesis 13:8. Also, in the New Testament, we find the Greek word philoneikia (φιλονεικία) which indicates a quarrel or dispute in Luke 22:24. In Romans 13:13 and 1 Corinthians 3:3 we find the word eris (ἔρις), which depicts altercation, strife, and discord or contentious disposition. Van Yperen reveals that "the word conflict is assumed everywhere and stated almost nowhere in Scripture." He cites Habakkuk 1:3 and Galatians 5:17 as the only places in each Testament, based on the New International Version, where the word actually appears.[1]

All human conflict should be understood in the context of the great cosmic controversy between good and evil. The Bible depicts a spiritual war in heaven, the result of Lucifer's disloyal and malicious actions against God, his Creator (Revelation 12:7-12). The conflict is represented as the manifestation of a rebellious spirit against the authority of God, with Lucifer desiring both the position and the authority of God as his own (Isaiah 14:12-15 and Ezekiel 28:11-19).

One of my favorite inspirational writers wrote:

> So long as all created beings acknowledged the allegiance of love, there was perfect harmony throughout the universe of God. It was the joy of the heavenly host to fulfill the purpose of their Creator. They delighted in reflecting His glory and showing forth His praise. And while love to God was supreme, love for

one another was confiding and unselfish. There was no note of discord to mar the celestial harmonies. But a change came over this happy state. There was one who perverted the freedom that God had granted to His creatures. Sin originated with him who, next to Christ, had been most honored of God and was highest in power and glory among the inhabitants of heaven. Lucifer, "son of the morning," was first of the covering cherubs, holy and undefiled. He stood in the presence of the great Creator, and the ceaseless beams of glory enshrouding the eternal God rested upon him. "Thus saith the Lord God; Thou sealest up the sum, full of wisdom, and perfect in beauty. Thou hast been in Eden the garden of God; every precious stone was thy covering. . . . Thou art the anointed cherub that covereth; and I have set thee so: thou wast upon the holy mountain of God; thou hast walked up and down in the midst of the stones of fire. Thou wast perfect in thy ways from the day that thou wast created, till iniquity was found in thee." Ezekiel 28:12-15.[2]

So there we have it! The spirit of pride and rebellion originated with Lucifer in the heavenly courts. Having lost the spiritual conflict, he was cast down to the earth as Scripture indicates (Rev. 12:10-13). Now the avowed enemy of God, this former highly exalted being set his sights on destroying humanity. Using the same cunning with which he misrepresented God's character and manipulated the angels, Satan launched his destructive plan to cause conflict and chaos among the inhabitants of this planet. While only two people occupied the earth, Satan artfully sowed the seeds of perpetual rebellion and conflict in the hearts of humankind. It may be noted in Gen.

3:8-10, that one of humanity's first reactions to their fall in Eden was to "hide" from God. This hiding, evasiveness, or withdrawal is indicative of a broken relationship. Thus, humans find themselves in conflict with God and His righteous principles. The great controversy which began in heaven has now come to earth, and all humanity is involved, not as mere spectators, but as participants. Humanity's separation from the Creator mimics Lucifer's separation from Him. Both are the result of disloyalty. The result is the same—broken relationships and a loss of harmony.

At the end of Genesis 1, the Creator had declared everything in the created world to be very good. Humankind had been created. The provisions for their habitation of the earth were perfect. Perfect order had been established. The fall of humanity (Genesis 3) caused a distortion of what God had intended. From open communion with God to withdrawal from God, humanity had fallen into a state of "not so good", which is effectively a reversal of Gen 1:31.

The great, continuing controversy between God and Satan therefore becomes the foundation, the source of all conflict. The great controversy motif is instinctively evident in every conflict situation. It is a contrary and destructive reality to the harmony and peace that the Creator had planned for humankind and the universe. Wars and strife between nations and individuals are mere microcosms of the cosmic controversy which started in heaven and was introduced to our planet by the fallen angel Lucifer, now called Satan (meaning enemy or adversary of God). It is against this backdrop that I make the following arguments, that: (1) conflict is universal and is inevitable as long as Satan and sin exist; (2) wherever there is conflict, it should be recognized that Satan is present and at work to divide and destroy; and (3) humankind in general, and Christians in particular, have a responsibility to learn how to prevent and resolve conflict, as far as is possible.

Scripture is quite clear that all conflict will one day be brought to an end (Rev 21:1-5), because Satan (the instigator of conflict) and all sinners will be destroyed (see John 8:28, 29 and Rev 20:5, 6). Until that time comes, Christian congregations that love and worship the Creator God have many biblical examples from which to extract important lessons and principles regarding both the causes and proper resolution of conflict. These principles need to be studied for the purpose of understanding and resolving congregational conflict.

Group Activities

(Get into groups of 3-4 people)

Discover: This activity requires vulnerability, great sensitivity, and confidentiality within the group. The purpose of this exercise is not to blame someone for a particular conflict occurrence, not to "try" the case within the group, but merely for participants to share their particular conflict experience and state how it impacted them.

Note: Group members who are listening should not only seek to hear the words, but also the heart of the person who is speaking. Question: What do you hear the person saying, as it pertains to the impact and effect of the situation upon them emotionally and spiritually, and the toll it took on their sense of dignity and integrity?

1. **For Pastors:** Take turns sharing a significant conflict event that occurred very early in your ministry. Talk about how the experience impacted and affected you emotionally and spiritually, and what effect it had on your sense of dignity, integrity and your courage to continue doing ministry.

2. **For Lay Members and Ministerial Students:** Share your brief story of a significant church conflict that you have witnessed or were involved in. How did it impact and affect

you emotionally and spiritually? What was your observation regarding the toll the issue had the congregation? How did it affect the pastor and his/her family?

3. **For Denominational Leaders:** In what ways can the process for installing new pastors in churches within your denomination/organization be improved to facilitate a smoother transition for both the congregation and the pastor? Do you have a system in place for de-briefing the outgoing pastor and briefing the incoming pastor before installation day? What kinds of training programs does your organization have in place to equip pastors in the art of conflict ministry?

Reflection Questions

1. How would you explain the reality of church conflict in the context of the cosmic controversy between God and Satan?

2. I stated that "All human conflict should be understood in the context of the great cosmic controversy between good and evil." How does this view cause you to re-think your attitude toward conflict, and those who you may be in conflict with?

3. What are the implications of a member reporting to you that "the people" are unhappy with your (or your pastor's) ministry? Describe how you would seek to address this non-specific complaint and deal with the matter of unidentified complainers. What potential snares exist, based on your reaction or lack of response?

Notes

1. Jim Van Yperen, *Making Peace: A Guide to Overcoming Church Conflict* (Chicago, IL: Moody Publishers, 2002), 94, 95.

2. Ellen G. White, *Patriarchs and Prophets* (1890; repr., Nampa, ID: Pacific Press, 1958), 35.

CHAPTER 2

Why So Many Toxic Churches and Angry Saints?

When I arrived at this next church under consideration, it was rather obvious from the very first day that there was much tension among the membership. I was the seventh pastor to be installed in twenty-three years! In my first week, I found that the local leadership was terribly fractured. There was open, well known and long-standing discord between some of the elders. The membership turnover rate had been historically high. There were four easily recognizable factions or cliques vying for the control of the church.

At least two rather assertive and very vocal members had major issues with certain theological teachings of the church. They defiantly and consistently promoted teachings that were not consistent with our faith. One of them had been elected an elder consistently for several years even though it was well known and documented that he pushed his disagreeable theological views upon the church through his private interactions and even from the pulpit.

One sister was so dominant, that even some of the men appeared to fear her. In fact, she assertively introduced herself to me in a manner that suggested to me that I needed to pay homage to her in order to be able to lead the church! When I did my due diligence and checked with previous pastors to learn as much as I could about the congregation, the very first pastor assigned to the church shared that the church had manifested a toxic character ever since the time of their initial organization! In other words, what I was seeing was nothing new, even though some of the people who were currently part of the problem, arrived, in some cases, years later. The church was located in a major town; however, the membership and attendance did not reflect the potential of the city for church growth. In fact, the church remained rather stagnant over the years.

By the time I arrived as the new pastor, it had become commonplace for certain of the members to arrogantly refer to the church as "our church" in a manner that was possessively suggestive. The sister who I previously mentioned wanted me to know that she was a "take charge" type of individual who did not need to wait on the pastor before acting as she saw fit! In that brief exchange, she also had some choice words about my predecessor, whom she clearly did not care for very much.

Another man had been allowed to serve as the head elder too many times and for far too long. He gave every pastor a hard time. This church was not a safe place for people seeking to have a meaningful encounter with God. Conflict on just about every level was rampant. Guests rarely returned repeatedly, choosing instead to travel to churches farther away, seeking a safe place to worship God.

Culturally (yes, churches develop cultures for how they do things), an "anything goes" mindset prevailed. Order and decency in church administration and operations, and respect for church polity and protocol seemed to be a foreign language. As far as responsibility for the spiritual, organizational, and dysfunctional state of the church went, the well-rehearsed argument over several years was that "the pastors who came here have been the problem" at this church. Of course, there was the silent minority who would privately express otherwise in hushed tones when the feared, dominant personalities were not within view.

Within two months of my arrival, the sister mentioned above sought to convince me and the church that I was the problem... in less than two months! That was a failed, but none-the-less damaging attempt to project the sins and shortcomings of the church upon yet another pastor. As you might imagine, this church caused me to pray like never before. This was a toxic church, and with the exception of a small minority, it was being overrun by some rather angry saints!

In this chapter, I will examine the various types of causes of conflict situations that I have observed in the Bible. These may be grouped under certain general headings or classifications of counsels and admonitions that may be of benefit to today's congregations. Here, I offer my reflections on these groupings. My classifications do not necessarily indicate an exhaustive list of possible headings. I will limit my discussion here to those groupings that formed the basis of my doctoral research, and which are mentioned below.

I have chosen to categorize my observations of "types of causes" of congregational conflict as follows: (1) rebellion and opposition to leadership, (2) when leadership issues cause church conflict, (3) the problem of personal greatness and pre-eminence, (4) failure to respect and celebrate cultural diversity, (5) theological disputes as a catalyst for conflict, (6) the consequences of disregard for protocol, and (7) mishandling of disagreements and misunderstandings.

Rebellion and Opposition to Leadership

Perhaps one of the clearest examples of rebellion against one of God's appointed spiritual leaders is the people's treatment of

Moses in the story of the Exodus. As recorded in various books of the Bible (Exodus, Leviticus, Numbers, and Deuteronomy), Moses was severely and constantly criticized, even verbally abused, for just about everything he did as their leader. His instructions were almost always second-guessed. There was open disagreement with him on almost every major directive that he gave. God, meanwhile, regarded the behavior of the people as not mere difference of opinion, but rebellion. What is amazing to me is that Moses' leadership was visibly and unmistakably affirmed by the LORD on several occasions, beginning with the plagues in Egypt, then confirmed by the Red Sea crossing, and the many miracles which were done in the wilderness. At a glance, one may fail to understand how the people could have missed the fact that Moses was God's man doing God's bidding. However, upon closer examination, there is a clear pattern of decided resistance among the Children of Israel. On every occasion that I have surveyed, God regards their actions as rebellion, not just against Moses, but against Himself.

In Numbers 14, God's view of the people's actions and attitudes comes into sharp focus. The text indicates that they complained and murmured against Moses. Verses 5-9 serve to demonstrate the spiritual reality of the matter. Joshua and Caleb, two of the spies who surveyed Canaan, cautioned the faithless and faultfinding throng against rebelling "against the Lord." The text indicates that these two men understood that Moses was not acting on his own volition. To them, Moses was the Lord's appointed leader, through whom He was directing Israel concerning what to do and where to go. It was the Lord who set Moses over them to carry out God's purpose of giving them the land of Canaan. They clearly saw Moses' leadership and God's leadership as one and the same.

To be sure, sometimes the problem in a church is due to the leader's fault. We will examine this scenario later in this book.

However, the Exodus story (as depicted in the book of Numbers) provides several examples of consequences resulting from rebellion against God-appointed, Spirit-led leaders. These consequences included: complainers dying of the plague with flesh between their teeth (11:31-34), leprosy brought upon Miriam for insubordination (12:4-15), extended wanderings in the wilderness by four decades (chap. 14) including warriors lost in battle because of the stubborn delay in inhabiting Canaan (14:39-45), rebels swallowed alive by the earth (16:32), rebels consumed by fire (v. 35), snake bites (21:6), and the most serious consequence of all -- the judgment of death upon all the Israelite pilgrims above twenty years old who left Egypt for Canaan. Keep in mind that this is not an exhaustive, but a representative list of consequences arising from the many occasions of rebellion and faithlessness in the Exodus narrative.

Today, resistance and rebellion against God-appointed leaders in the congregational setting are similarly real and damaging. There are many books on the Christian literature market that address this issue. The problem is widespread. Many congregations have plateaued or declined, and some have been nearly decimated because of congregational conflict and its stagnating and destructive effect. The Exodus experiences show how a relatively small, discordant faction (the "mixed multitude") within the congregation can quickly and negatively influence and impact the entire congregation. They can influence enough people in the congregation against their pastors and other leaders to cause a significant disruption. This activity leads toward open rebellion, which can seriously cripple the church.

Scripture indicates that there was a "mixed multitude" within the congregation of the Children of Israel during their wilderness sojourn. Of these, Ellen White writes:

> The mixed multitude that came up with the Israelites
> from Egypt were a source of continual temptation and
> trouble. They professed to have renounced idolatry,
> and to worship the true God; but their early education
> and training had molded their habits and characters,
> and they were more or less corrupted with idolatry
> and with irreverence for God. They were oftenest the
> ones to stir up strife, and were the first to complain,
> and they leavened the camp with their idolatrous
> practices and their murmurings against God.[1]

The mixed multitude was without excuse, however, concerning their arrogance, faithlessness and rebellious actions. Though they were not Israelites, they were quite aware, as were the Israelites, that it was Jehovah who was leading them on their journey. There was constant, reliable, visible, physical evidence of this fact. The Egyptians were idolaters who worshipped images in order to "see" their gods. Their religion was by sight, not by faith. Their confidence rested entirely in what they could see. The Children of Israel had apparently accepted this way of thinking as well, during their sojourn in Egypt. No wonder then, that God would provide visible, physical evidence of His leading: "God Himself directed the Israelites in all their travels. The place of their encampment was indicated by the descent of the pillar of cloud; and so long as they were to remain in camp, the cloud rested over the tabernacle."[2]

There is an important principle to note here. In situations where the members of the church complain and rebel, it is often viewed as merely a movement against, or dissatisfaction with the pastor. The pastor happens to be the leader who the people are able to see. However, what the story of the Exodus shows, is that Moses was not the one directing the journeys of Israel; God Himself was their leader. He was the One directing the very path they were taking.

Moses was merely carrying out the mandate of God as revealed to him. This is an important theological insight that is often missed or misunderstood by some church members. Complaining, revolting, and refusing to cooperate with clearly God-appointed church leaders is a more serious spiritual matter than most realize.

God appears in the Exodus narrative and takes strong exception to the attitudes and behaviors of the people that in any way hinder the leadership of His servants whom He chooses to carry out His purpose. The lesson here may be summed up like this: God leads His people through leaders of His own choosing. These leaders are to be obedient to Him, faithfully carrying out His mandate. Meanwhile, the congregation is to show deference (be respectful and positively responsive in their cooperation) to the appointed servants of God.

When Leadership Issues Cause Church Conflict

Moses is described in Scripture as the meekest man who ever lived. "Now the man Moses was very humble, more than all men who were on the face of the earth" (Num. 12:3). With such an incredible endorsement, how could Moses have experienced so much congregational conflict in his ministry as the spiritual leader of Israel? It seems logical that church members would respond positively to a leader who, by all biblical accounts, was almost perfect, and who had been shown to be in direct contact with God.

What may be clearly understood from this reality is that the character, personality or temperament of the leader (contrary to what is so often claimed) does not exempt him or her from conflict. No amount of humility that Moses possessed prevented the people from attacking him and constantly complaining about his leadership. In other words, it does not matter who the leader is, or what is their leadership style, "conflict is inevitable for leaders, and it exists at the root of some of their best ideas and at the core of many of their worst failures."[3] In fact, trouble at times may mean that the spiritual leader is in fact, faithfully fulfilling God's will.[4] This view may not receive the endorsement of some, but failing to accept this fact makes it no less true.

I have had experiences where I was operating out of a highly developed and recognized area of strength (church leadership), yet was vehemently criticized by a small group of detractors while doing critical transformational ministry. It was during one of these seasons of unmerciful onslaught against my leadership (ability and direction) that I concluded that Satan doesn't only attack pastors in our areas of limitation, flaw, or weakness, but also in our areas of strength. The purpose for this, I reason, is to cause the servants of God to become disillusioned and discouraged. If the pastor is being criticized when operating in his weakness, but is also fiercely criticized when operating in his strength, he could become discouraged, thinking and feeling as though he has no ministry value and therefore has nothing positive to contribute to the building up the kingdom of God. In short, he may get to the place where he starts feeling like an abject failure as a pastor, unable to satisfy the expectations of anyone.

There are those times however, when damaging congregational conflict is, in fact, either caused or escalated by the pastor. Suffice it to say, and it is generally understood, that like all other human beings, pastors do have strengths, weaknesses, limitations, and flaws. That being said, there are some specific types of personal baggage that will almost always trigger conflict. Susek identifies two of these types of baggage as (1) destructive family backgrounds and (2) unresolved psycho-social needs.[5]

Reflecting on these two concepts, I agree with Susek that the spiritual leader's psycho-social needs are best met by God Himself, or by a qualified person who functions in a professional capacity. Attempts by a pastor to extract personal sympathy or any other form of emotional support for the satisfaction or fulfillment of personal psychological or psycho-social needs from the congregation may trigger unnecessary conflicts as the members begin to question their leader's credibility and emotional stability. Self-knowledge and clearly defined accountability measures would be advisable for any pastor, seeing that there are so many occasions for compromised behavior as a result of emotional imbalance.

Christian leaders cannot be too careful in the matter of sorting out their own feelings and psycho-social issues. Failure to do so can lead to terrible consequences for the pastor and for the congregation as a whole. This is probably more so true in the area of pastoral counseling of parishioners than any other situation, where "many pastors fail to recognize their own inner signals."[6] Unhealthy dependencies between pastor and congregant may form in cases where the pastor is not emotionally and psycho-socially well.

King Saul appears to have had a psychological problem (1 Sam 16:14-22). The king is described in the text as a man with a distressed spirit. White indicates that this disturbed state of mind was brought on by an evil spirit, and that David was brought in "to soothe the mind of the troubled monarch till the evil spirit should depart from him."[7] With this psychological imbalance, it is understandable that he would behave in the manner that he did, especially in response to the people's favoring of David. The youngster did nothing wrong to offend the king; however, the king became angry and violent toward him.

As the leader, Saul should have provided inspiration and moral support to those who served under him, but the king was psychologically unwell and distressed. David was brought in to minister to this particular unresolved need. The king became dependent upon David's music to calm his maniacal emotions. He apparently failed to depend on the Lord to be his helper. Leaders who are emotionally or psycho-socially unbalanced, risk escalating conflict and may contribute to "resentment, alienation, and eventually resistance from those on the losing side."[8]

Saul's irritated nerves got the better of him, and in his insecurity and jealousy, he attempted to kill David on various occasions. His emotional state and personal insecurities led him to pursue and persecute David, a subordinate. Saul's actions were clearly irrational. The narrative shows that emotional instability in leaders can trigger conflict with church members because of how leaders sometimes mishandle their own, intra-personal issues. The Christian leader needs to be emotionally and psycho-socially secure in Christ. It is only the leader's personal relationship and complete dependence upon God and His grace that will enable him or her to lead with integrity, and maintain a focus of helping the people, rather than seeking emotional help from the people.

Leadership issues are not limited to pastors. I estimate that more than 90% of church conflicts originate within the leadership core, among the pastor and the local leadership team. Sometimes there is conflict between the pastor and elders or the church board or the board of trustees, depending on the organizational structure of the church. Other times, the conflict occurs among the local leadership core, minus the pastor, such as conflict among elders or conflict among the trustees. It should not be assumed that leadership issues are primarily the fault of the pastor. In fact, I would argue that most of the conflict in the local church is not caused by the pastor. Let me explain this view.

The one person who has the most riding on the success of the church is the pastor. No other member of the body of Christ is as professionally and otherwise benefitted by the church's success. Contra-wise, no other member of the body of Christ pays more for the church's failures or perceived failures, professionally and otherwise. Pastors therefore have a vested interest in doing all they can to insure the success of the church. The pastor's ministry will be judged by the success, or the real or perceived failure of the church. The trustees and the elders do not have the same burden of accountability or scrutiny; although they are not completely immune from blame should the church appear to be failing. Think about it... the pastor is usually the one who receives a salary, which comes with an expectation of care for the church. He or she is held to a higher standard than which volunteer members are normally held to.

While it is true that there are some "bad apples" in the pastoral ministry, I am prepared to go "out on a limb" to say that the vast majority of pastors are people who are doing their best good, by the grace of God, to serve their congregations in the manner and direction they sense that God is leading them. Leadership issues almost always trickle down through the leadership structure to the membership as a whole. It is imperative therefore, that there is a code of honor and decency within the leadership team concerning how disagreements are handled. There are also frequent occurrences when ego and the ambition for personal greatness and pre-eminence come in among the members of the church and cause major conflict.

The Problem of Personal Greatness and Pre-eminence

There was conflict among Jesus' twelve disciples. They had misunderstood the nature of Christ's kingdom.[9] The prophets and rabbis had, for many years, taught the restoration of their nation. With this view of a literal restoration of the kingdom to Israel, accompanied by an intense longing for deliverance from their Roman oppressors, the disciples were motivated to secure positions of honor for themselves. They argued about who should be the greatest among them (Mark 9:34; Luke 9:46). Jesus responded by likening greatness to servant-hood and humility. The desire for pre-eminence has often been a trigger for conflict, both in the secular world and in the church. Among the closest followers of Christ, selfish desires, jealousy, and ambition invariably led to strife.

It was during the heart-searching preparation for the baptism of the Holy Spirit that the disciples realized their error. They were changed. "No longer were they ignorant and uncultured. No longer were they a collection of independent units or discordant, conflicting elements. No longer were their hopes set on worldly greatness."[10]

The quest for personal greatness and self-exaltation, however, did not originate on earth, but in heaven with Lucifer. In Eden, disguised as a serpent, Satan enticed the woman with the promise that "you will be like God" (Gen. 3:5). This statement inspired what would become mankind's all-consuming passion - to be great, superior, exalted above their fellow human beings. Humility was relegated instead of celebrated, and has ever since been degraded and devalued as a result.

As seen earlier in this book regarding the narrative of the Exodus, Korah, Dathan, and Abiram arrogantly sought to oppose and exalt themselves against Moses, God's chosen leader. These men thus became the cause and instigators of destructive conflict in the camp of the Israelites. Their attitudes and actions brought terrible consequences upon themselves and upon those who followed their evil example. Lucifer too, had indulged self-exaltation, even though he was already the most highly exalted of all created beings! His quest to obtain God's glory for himself caused great disharmony and disruption in the perfect atmosphere and precinct of heaven.[11]

Failure to Respect and Celebrate Cultural Diversity

Cultural differences have probably been a challenge for human relationships since the very early history of humanity.[12] With the introduction of different languages at Babel (Gen. 11) and the subsequent scattering of people throughout the earth, cultures probably began emerging in a more structured manner. Just as individuals are different, people groups also have unique qualities and norms that identify them by a systematic way of thinking and doing. Religion appears to have been a predominant differentiator between peoples of the Bible times. The Hebrew people were distinct from other peoples, not only because they worshiped Jehovah while most worshiped heathen gods, but also because they were regarded as a "special" people who came into existence because of God's covenant with Abraham (Gen. 12-18).

The existence and reality of diverse cultures is further complicated by their sub-groups or sub-cultures. A sub-culture is defined as "a group having social, economic, ethnic, or other traits distinctive enough to distinguish it from others within the same culture or society."[13] The existence of cultures and sub-cultures additionally brings into focus the necessity of understanding and appreciating cultural diversity, both in society and in the church. The acceptance of cultural diversity is a Christian principle (see Acts 10). This principle points to at least two important essentials: (1) How to achieve and preserve unity in the context of such diversity, and (2) Understanding that the nature of cultural diversity makes uniformity of thoughts and actions both impractical and humanly impossible.

So should culture matter, seeing that the Church is one body? It would be a mistake to assume that the natural realities and challenges brought about by cultural diversity would somehow be eliminated by the fact that the congregation is the body of Christ. This belief or expectation indicates a rather simplistic view of what cultural diversity is and does. On this point, Hohnberger offers that:

> Unity never comes as a result of membership in a church, never as the result of joining a ministry or institution, and never as the result of agreeing to certain truths. Unity comes only as a result of different people from different backgrounds and, yes, even with different biases joining themselves to Jesus Christ. Unity is experienced only to the degree to which we are united to Jesus.[14]

I agree with Hohnberger that church membership alone, or even the acceptance of vital doctrines, cannot take the place of personal conversion and transformation in order that naturally carnal minded people can "dwell together in unity" (Ps 133:1). Menjares holds that "the overwhelming testimony of scripture is that the church is to be a multi-cultural, multi-national, and multilingual gathering of believers."[15] Oosterwal opines that communication is impacted by cultural differences, that the varying values in people's basic assumptions are shaped by their cultural background; and that these assumptions shape their perceptions of reality and their views of right and wrong.[16] Jesus is concerned about the unity of the Church. He prayed that his followers would be one (John 17:17). However, I rather doubt that He intended uniformity in how people perceive God, and how we express our gratitude to Him through worship, given our individual experiences and spiritual needs, as well as the fact that people's cultural backgrounds vary so widely.

Much biblical space is dedicated to outlining and expressing God's will for human relationships. This is also true for the amount of divine instruction concerning what to do when relationships do go wrong. Cultural and sub-cultural differences are common causes of interpersonal conflict and church fights. These differences show up in various aspects and times of congregational life, such as: worship and music preference; the why, how, and when to implement change; the degree of involvement of members in the decision-making process of the church; the extent to which both clergy and lay members engage in the leadership process of the local church; and the role and responsibility of various clergy and lay members in the leadership process.

Sometimes cultural differences manifest themselves along the lines of gender. One notable example of this is the current debate in the some sectors of the Christian Church on the question of women in ministry in general, and their ordination to the pastoral ministry in particular. I hold that there is no biblical ground for excluding women from the gospel ministry, with ordination, and access to all the associated rights, responsibilities, and privileges of full-time clergy. I view the debate strictly as a cultural one, based upon the ancient patriarchal norms of the Jewish people, and of some cultures today. In some congregations, women are not allowed to be elders, based upon the perception that it would be wrong, or worse, that it is a sin to allow women to serve as spiritual leaders (see Joel 2:28, 29).

Another sensitive way in which culture impacts the church is the debate about music in worship. This debate tends to center on the question of what is considered to be appropriate church music. Significant differences exist in this dialog between the old and the young, between races, and between ethnic groups. In my experience and observation, the responses to this question are culture based, seeing that the Bible does not specifically address what worship music should look and sound like.

Seeing that there is so much opportunity for conflict, I am of the view that a sound theology of worship is essential for harmony among the congregation and for the moving of the Spirit to be effectual during corporate worship. Segler puts it this way, "Worship should be regulated and determined by doctrine."[17] In this, I agree with him. Many cultural conflicts have crippled untold numbers of churches over the question of worship, and music in worship. The strongest viewpoints which I have heard in my own experience have not necessarily been Bible based, but rather the expression of opinions and traditions. In other words, the cultural norms and expressions of the strongest or most vocal members of the church gets expressed and implemented. Meanwhile, the smaller or "weaker" sub-groups are shut out or shut down, and may resort to open defiance or the tactics of subtle insurgency in order to assert their desires. Either way, we are headed for congregational conflict.

In some churches, certain instruments, such as the drum, are debated or even forbidden. In all my years of being a Christian, I have yet to hear a Bible text appropriately quoted and faithfully exegeted in support of such a position. Doctrinal instruction may go a long way in helping congregations to properly understand the difference between personal preferences, traditions, and right versus wrong. Proper instruction would also teach tolerance and acceptance of other cultures, and an appreciation of their norms of worship. Dudley Weeks argues for caution in how people manage their perceptions, because "conflict usually involves a struggle between absolutes, such as right and wrong and good and evil."[18]

Theological Disputes as the Catalyst for Conflict

When I arrived as the new pastor at Church X, only a few people attended the weekly adult Sabbath School. It did not take long to learn why. For years, the adult Sabbath School class had developed a reputation for being an atmosphere of heated, distracting theological arguments. Some who ventured to attend were often left shaking their heads in bewilderment. A certain member had made it his weekly routine to cause chaos, arguing vehemently with the Bible class teacher, usually about personal, controversial pet peeves, regardless of the topic of the scheduled lesson. It soon became apparent to me that this member had a psychological need to attract attention to himself, albeit negative, probably because of some disorder or insecurity. Every week, without fail, his incredulous and rather assertive theological remarks would derail the lesson that members had studied in their quarterlies. The problem was chronic.

The most difficult challenge dealing with this member was that after several one-to-one and group meetings that I had with him and with the elders, the situation did not improve. Not only that, but I discovered that at least three of my predecessors had talked with him about this conduct, to no avail. To add to my dilemma, he was also serving as an elder of the church! Obviously, that was not acceptable to me, nor supportive of my work as the pastor. I therefore removed him from the speaking roster, and instructed that he should not be assigned to teach the Sabbath School. I then advised the nominating committee later that year that he should not be considered for any office in the church. The nominating committee was happy for the leadership I showed on the issue. For years, the members had felt paralyzed by a fear of conflict, powerless to take action in the case of someone who so flagrantly violated the harmony and peace of the church. Unruly members holding churches hostage is not at all rare.

Theological harmony is not optional in the church. Paul advocated that there is "one faith" (Eph. 4:5). The brother in the above example eventually stopped attending Church X. He was of the view that he had a right to his opinions, and even had the right to preach those views to the members and guests of the church. Though the contrary teachings of this man were a constant cause of concern among the membership, when I took action to remove him from positions of influence in the church, some came to his defense, arguing that I was denying him his freedom of speech! I had made it clear that the decision to discontinue his teaching privileges was for the sake of harmony and the preservation of doctrinal unity in the church. His few supporters angrily attacked my character and credibility, and questioned my authority to "sit him down." This issue brings into focus the question of how to reconcile the tension between the secular Bill of Rights and the right of religious organizations to establish and protect religious beliefs and practice.

While at Miletus, Paul sent for the elders from Ephesus. He charged them to remain faithful to the Word of God, and warned them that after his departure, false teachers would seek to come in among them and devour the congregations with spurious doctrines (see Acts 20:1-32). The great apostle, in his second letter to Timothy, urged him to be faithful to the Word, and to preach nothing else (2 Tim. 3:10-4:5). Paul refers to baseless theological disputes as "vain babblings" because they profit nothing (2 Tim. 2:14-18).

Ellen White encouraged the continuous, prayerful study of the Scriptures, and that the student of the Word should, in humility, accept advancing light. She also cautioned against error:

> If a brother is teaching error, those who are in responsible positions ought to know it; and if he is teaching truth, they ought to take their stand at his side. We should all know what is being taught among us; for if it is truth, we need to know it. The Sabbath school teacher needs to know it, and every Sabbath school scholar ought to understand it. We are all under obligation to God to understand what He sends us. He has given directions by which we may test every doctrine—"To the law and to the testimony: if

they speak not according to this word, it is because there is no light in them." But if it is according to this test, do not be so full of prejudice that you cannot acknowledge a point simply because it does not agree with your ideas.[19]

Keeping in mind that worship is at the heart of the great controversy (when Lucifer sought to obtain the glory that is due to God alone), there can be no tolerance of contrary teachings being urged upon the church. It was by twisting the Word of God that the serpent was able to deceive the woman in Eden (Gen. 3:1-6). Doctrines are important. Doctrinal unity and correctness is even more important. People live by their beliefs, so it is critical that only truth be presented and accepted, as this will invariably affect the life.

When a doctrinal dispute erupted in the early church, the apostles, being led of the Holy Spirit, wisely decided to meet in Jerusalem to pray together, and settle the matter collectively and harmoniously (Acts 15:1-29). They did not engage in theological one-upmanship. They realized the necessity of moving in concert with one another under the leading of the Holy Spirit to prevent a schism in the body. Doctrinal unity promotes congregational unity.

The book of Revelation emphasizes that terrible judgments of God will be poured out upon those who reject His Word and live outside of His revealed will. In the apocalyptic narrative, the Lord also stressed the importance of what John the writer was shown to be "the everlasting gospel" (Rev 14:6, 7). The word "everlasting" (from the Greek "aionios" αἰώνιος) is used only here in Scripture in connection with the gospel. There is only one gospel, and it will continue as long as time exists.[20] There is a need for the Church to work toward theological harmony. Protocol (the established principles and procedures that determine how and by whom functions are carried out) is another important source of potential and frequent conflict in the church.

The Consequences of Disregard for Protocol

The matter of protocol in handling the affairs of the church is an important subject. I have seen many congregational conflicts occur as a result of disregard for proper protocol. God is a God of order (1 Cor. 14:33). He requires system and order in His Church.

Without organization and intelligent procedures for handling the things of the gospel, utter chaos would result. It must be noted that the Bible does not provide specific procedures for doing most church functions of administration and ministry as practiced today. What it provides are mostly broad principles that must be developed and applied to the contemporary, and often, local context. This is a good thing, seeing that as times change, the methods for doing many things in life also change. Doctrines are developed from the unchanging Word of God, but, the methods of delivering and administering the mission of the Church must be subject to constant review and updating.

McSwain and Treadwell make a good case when they talk about the importance of how a church is organized, with respect to the impact that the organizational structure will have on the potential of the church to fall into conflict. This is mainly due to the ease with which the structure allows effective communication and decision-making to take place.

Some organizational structures contribute more to competition between departments or ministries than to effective communication. In addition, an emphasis on structure that is not balanced by adequate and clearly thought out and agreed-upon processes is prone to generate conflict.[21] In other words, all conflict in churches does not stem from interpersonal issues, but also non-personal causes.

Quite often in churches, however, conflict occurs because of the intentional violation of established protocols. In one case, a ministry leader violated the clearly articulated protocol of not inviting anyone to be a guest speaker at the church, for any reason, until and unless I had approved such a move. In fact, the protocol of our denomination is that only the assigned pastor can invite someone to speak. The assigned pastor is responsible for the pulpit, not the church board, or even the church as a whole. The local conference holds the pastor (supported by the church) responsible for the protection of the pulpit. This protocol has several benefits to the church, including safeguarding the pulpit from unauthorized persons, protecting the membership from contrary teachings, respecting the fact that the pastor is responsible for the pulpit, and demonstrating the local church's support for denominational policy. A ministry leader or officer may recommend, but it is the pastor who invites speakers.

On three different occasions, I had re-iterated the protocol in the board meetings, of which the above-mentioned individual was a member. Nonetheless, this ministry leader chose to defy my authority, disregard conference policy, and unilaterally invited an outside person to speak for the divine service on a certain Sabbath when her ministry would be highlighted. This was done without my prior knowledge or approval.

As if her conduct was not bad enough, the member then sent an e-mail to the entire membership, announcing that the unauthorized person would be the guest speaker for that ministry's special day! I found out about it at the same time, and in the same way, as did all the members of the church—through the e-mail. This was a blatant breach of protocol by a defiant member of the congregation.

Needless to say, I disallowed the speaker. I then cancelled the special day altogether when the erring member became more defiant and belligerent. I further instructed her that it was her responsibility to inform the intended speaker, whom she had invited, that he was not authorized to speak at the church, as I had not invited him to do so. Amazingly, the intended speaker was also a pastoral colleague, someone who should have seen to it that proper protocol was followed. He should have known better than to accept a speaking invitation from a lay member of a church where a pastor has been assigned by the governing conference. This was an unnecessary conflict that the church was subjected to by a reckless and disrespectful member. Some of her family members obviously sided with her, based on their view that I should not have cancelled the "speaker," in spite of her blatant disregard for my responsibility over the congregation. Let me be clear - the pastor's first responsibility is to protect the church (meaning the people). That includes situations like this. My duty as the pastor is to lead the church in an orderly and safe manner.

I am reminded of a case in the ministry of Moses, God's servant. It is the narrative of blatant disregard for God's protocol regarding the offering of sacrifices on the altar. In the story (see Lev. 9:22-10:7) of Nadab and Abihu (Moses' two nephews, the sons of Aaron), they foolishly offered unauthorized or "strange" fire before the Lord. Their thinking was that God would or should accept their folly. Instead, God sent fire from above and consumed them before all Israel for their rather presumptuous sin.

Bible parallels of the disregard for protocol, such as told in this narrative, show God's serious insistence concerning order and decency, and proper regard for organizational protocols that promote harmony among His people. Those who have the privilege of leading out in any aspect of God's work would do well to take these admonitions seriously. Another example of the importance of following proper protocol in holy things is the transporting of the Ark of the

Covenant on a cart. God's judgment upon Uzzah was immediate and decisive (2 Sam. 6:1-13), for daring to violate the well-known rule of respect for how to handle the things of God.

Mishandling of Disagreements and Misunderstandings

A theology of conflict must necessarily include the appropriate biblical principle which states "let nothing be done through strife or vain glory" (Phil. 2:3). While occasional personal disagreements are normal and may even be healthy, this text admonishes us to glorify God in all things, which would include how we handle disputes and disagreements. Lucifer sought to undermine God's glory and authority. He envied God's power. The consequences of Satan's covetousness serve as important lessons for God's people today.

The apostle says, "But you are a chosen generation, a royal priesthood, a holy nation, His own special people, that you may proclaim the praises of Him who called you out of darkness into His marvelous light" (1 Pet. 2:9, 10). It should be noted here that the admonition is to do the opposite of what Lucifer did in heaven. God's glory is why He is worshipped, and He is glorified when we worship Him. The glory belongs to God alone. His people glorify Him through healthy, harmonious inter-personal relationships.

God should be glorified even when His people have disagreements among them. God is not angry when we disagree. The problem is with how we choose to handle our disagreements. Unfortunately, in too many cases of disagreement, God is not glorified. Disagreements are mishandled and deteriorate into fighting or in-fighting among the people of God. This in-fighting causes a state of damaging conflict to prevail in the church. Ricki Lee Brooks advances the view that "the answer then for differences is not fighting. Neither is it to cover them or hide them. Rather, differences should be mutually worked out until a sound resolution is found."[22] Mishandled disagreement is often characterized by accusing and counter-accusing by the disputing parties. The goal of glorifying God must therefore be included in how we relate to conflict.

The apostle Paul appears to have had cause to plead with the members of the church at Ephesus concerning their interpersonal relationships. He admonished them to deal with misunderstandings and conflict appropriately. His plea serves as recognition that church members will sometimes be angry because of relational breakdowns; however, the following biblical text admonishes persons in disputes and conflict to deal with their differences and misunderstandings in a manner that honors God. He makes this case well:

> Therefore, putting away lying, let each one of you speak truth with his neighbor, for we are members of one another. Be angry, and do not sin; do not let the sun go down on your wrath, nor give place to the devil. Let him who stole steal no longer, but rather let him labor, working with his hands what is good, that he may have something to give him who has need. Let no corrupt word proceed out of your mouth, but what is good for necessary edification, that it may impart grace to the hearers. And do not grieve the Holy Spirit of God, by whom you were sealed for the day of redemption. Let all bitterness, wrath, anger, clamor, and evil speaking be put away from you, with all malice. And be kind to one another, tenderhearted, forgiving one another, even as God in Christ forgave you (Eph. 4:25-32).

In their expression of anger during conflict or disputes, people sometimes sin. Sin may be expressed by being untruthful; hence the text admonishes conflicted parties to speak the truth. Conflicted persons may become resentful as a result of anger; therefore the text calls for speaking not only the truth, but doing so in love. There is also the danger of the offender being unrepentant or the offended being unforgiving.

Paul cautions his readers to avoid prolonging their anger toward one another. Prolonged anger may turn into wrath. Paul urges the speedy resolution of disputes. His use of the expression "do not let the sun go down" is obviously an exhortation to quickly settle differences, rather than a concern for the time of day that settlement is achieved. Surely, anger arising from serious difference or dispute can occur after the sun has already gone down!

In the text, the terms "be angry" and "sin not" are in the imperative mood. They are commands. This appears inconsistent at first glance; therefore, a closer examination of the text is warranted. A commentary on the text offers that:

> Various suggestions have been made in an attempt to avoid the implication of a command to be angry, none of them satisfactory. The simplest solution seems to be to regard the anger here spoken of as a righteous indignation. A Christian who is not aroused to the point of indignation by manifest wrongs and injustices may be insensitive to some things that ought to concern him. Righteous indignation has a most important function in stimulating men in the battle against evil. Jesus was not angered by any personal affront, but by hypocritical challenges to God and injustices done to others. . . Justifiable anger is directed against the wrong act without animosity toward the wrongdoer. To be able to achieve the two

is a supremely great Christian achievement. . . A warning is issued lest justifiable anger lead to feelings of personal resentment, vindictiveness, and loss of control.[23]

This is a plausible explanation of the text, given the imperative mood of the elements involved. It is apparent that Paul was by no means advocating interpersonal animosity or the bitterness which typically characterizes congregational conflict. In fact, one may infer from the text that it is desirable for Christians to be righteously vexed about damaging conflict or other threats that negatively affect the church.

Jesus clearly articulates how His followers should address issues and disputes with one another (Matt. 18:15; Luke 17:3, 4). The text indicates Christ's will, in that interpersonal disputes and conflict should be settled in the one-to-one forum where Christ-like conversation, confession, and conclusion of the difference or hurt best occurs. A broader understanding of the responsibility of both the offender and the offended in conflict is discussed later in this book.

Discussion Questions

Ministerial students and pastors:

This activity requires vulnerability, great sensitivity, and confidentiality within the group.

1. In groups of 3-4, discuss (and record the main points of your group discussion) the fact that pastors bring not only strengths, but also weaknesses, limitations and flaws to the pastoral function. How should this reality impact how the pastor handles disagreements with parishioners?

2. In your group, discuss the protocol regarding the pastor's role in the safeguard of the pulpit. Be sure to include the idea of some that the church is a democracy and that members should be allowed to make certain decisions as they see fit.

3. Church members: How do you view my response to the member who invited an unauthorized speaker to the church?

4. Denominational leaders: What can or should be done from the denomination's perspective to help prevent incidents such as the member who felt that she had the right to invite any speaker without the pastor's knowledge or approval?

Group Activities

1. Role Play: Appoint someone in your group to be the conference president, the ministerial director, and the pastor of the local church. If there is another group member, appoint him or her to be a church member. Have a discussion at the conference office about the importance of proper protocol in selecting and inviting speakers to the church.

2. Make a list of items that pertain to pastoral administration. Write down specific protocols that you may need to share with your church board about how you would like them to relate to these aspects of your responsibility. Make sure the protocols are not simply based upon your personal preference or pet peeve, but upon biblical principles and conference policy. Keep the principle of "best practices" in mind as you complete this exercise. Discuss your list with your group.

Notes

1. F. Brown, S. Driver and C. Briggs, *The Brown-Driver-Briggs Hebrew and English Lexicon* (1906; repr., Peabody, MA: Hendrickson Publishers, 1999), 936.

2. Ibid., 937.

3. Unless otherwise indicated, all Bible references in this paper will be taken from the New King James Version (NKJV). Where texts are used in quotations, the quoted version of the text is preserved.

4. Wesley J. Perschbacher, ed., *The New Analytical Greek Lexicon* (1990; repr., Peabody, MA: Hendrickson Publishers, 1999), 429.

5. Ibid., 172.

6. Jim Van Yperen, *Making Peace: A Guide to Overcoming Church Conflict* (Chicago, IL: Moody Publishers, 2002), 94, 95.

7. Ellen G. White, *Patriarchs and Prophets* (1890; repr., Nampa, ID: Pacific Press, 1958), 34.

8. White, *Patriarchs and Prophets,* 35.

9. Ibid.

10. F. Brown, S. Driver and C. Briggs, *The Brown-Driver-Briggs Hebrew and English Lexicon,* 285.

11. White, *Patriarchs and Prophets,* 408.

12. Ibid., 376.

13. Craig E. Runde and Tim A. Flanagan, *Becoming a Conflict Competent Leader: How You and Your Organization can Manage Conflict Effectively* (San Francisco, CA: John Wiley & Sons, 2007), 1.

14. Ron Susek, *Firestorm: Preventing and Overcoming Church Conflict* (Grand Rapids, MI: Baker Books, 1999), 71.

15. Ibid., 81-89.

16. James J. North Jr., "The Minister as a Counselor," in *The Adventist Minister,* ed. C. Raymond Holmes and Douglas Kilcher (Berrien Springs, MI: Andrews University Press, 1991), 92.

17. White, *Patriarchs and Prophets*, 643.

18. Runde and Flanagan, *Becoming a Conflict Competent Leader*, 35.

19. "Christ's Kingdom," *SDA Bible Commentary*, ed. Francis D. Nichol (1956; repr., Washington, DC: Review and Herald, 1980), 6:122.

20. Ellen G. White, *The Acts of the Apostles* (Nampa, ID: Pacific Press, 1911), 45.

21. White, *Patriarchs and Prophets*, 36.

22. I have defined culture as: A norm by which people identify with, and demonstrate that they belong to a particular group, based upon ethnicity, language, race, age, vocation, or other identifiable group classification. These norms may be expressed through language, music, religious beliefs and practices, social traditions, etc.

23. Dictionary.com, s.v. "Sub-culture," http://dictionary.reference.com/ browse/ sub-culture?s=t (accessed May 8, 2012).

24. Jim Hohnberger, with Tim and Julie Canuteson, *It's About People: How to Treat Others Especially Those We Disagree With, the Way Jesus Treats Us* (Nampa, ID: Pacific Press, 2003), 88.

25. Pete C. Menjares, "Is There a Biblical Basis for Encouraging Diversity?" 26 April 2010, http://unityinchristmagazine.com/theology/is-there-a-biblical-basis-for-encouraging-diversity (accessed May 8, 2012).

26. Gottfried Oosterwal, "Leaders and Cross-Cultural Communication: Communicating Across Cultural Boundaries," in *Embracing Diversity: How to Understand and Reach People of all Cultures*, ed. Leslie N. Pollard (Hagerstown, MD: Review and Herald, 2000), 22.

27. Franklin M. Segler, rev. by Randall Bradley, *Understanding, Preparing for, and Practicing Christian Worship* (Nashville: Broadman & Holman Publishers, 1996), 47.

28. Dudley Weeks, *The Eight Essential Steps to Conflict Resolution* (New York: Penguin Putnam, 1992), 9.

29. Ellen G. White, *Testimonies to Ministers and Gospel Workers* (1923; repr., Mountain View, CA: Pacific Press, 1962), 110.

30. "Everlasting Gospel," *SDA Bible Commentary*, 7:827.

31. Larry McSwain and William Treadwell Jr., *Conflict Ministry in the Church* (Hagerstown, MD: Review and Herald Graphics, 1997), 25-26.

32. Ricki Lee Brooks, *Let's Stop the Fighting: A Biblical Approach for Working Out Our Differences* (Silverdale, WA: Sound Communication, 2012), 36-37.

33. "Be angry" and "Sin not," *SDA Bible Commentary*, 6:1027.

34. Brooks, *Let's Stop the Fighting,* 13-14.

35. Ken Sande, *The Peace Maker: A Biblical Guide to Resolving Personal Conflict* (Grand Rapids, MI: Baker Books, 2004), 47-50.

CHAPTER 3

Hallelujah in the Midst of Hell: Divine Reassurance for the Church

W e've all heard it said over and over, that "united we stand, but a house divided will fall." This is also true for the church.

We are living in a time when more and more people are turning their backs on the church. We often hear folks say, "I don't believe in religion" or "I don't have to go to church to be saved." There are all kinds of opinions regarding the church. There are opinions about what the church is, what the church in not, what the church is for, and even diverse opinions about who the church is for. Then, there are opinions about what the church should believe and teach, opinions about whether or not the church has the right to determine who joins or to remove people from its membership, and opinions about how the financial resources that come into the church should be utilized. I could go on and on, sharing the multitude of views and arguments about the church. However, that would be an exercise in futility. I would submit that if one really wants to understand the church, such an inquiry should begin with Jesus. A very familiar scripture in Matthew 16 shows that the church has a sure foundation, Jesus Christ Himself. "Upon this Rock," is where the church is built!

A correct theology of the Church is absolutely essential for understanding why the church is important to God and to the Christian. There are three essential facts that set the Church apart from any other entity in the world. These three important realities must be embraced in order that those who subscribe to the ideal of the Church will find fulfilment and meaning in this endeavor of being church members and leaders: (1) Jesus founded the Church upon Himself; (2) Jesus prayed that the Church would be united; and (3) there are biblically established qualifiers that determine the parameters of what makes the Church the Church.

It's Built Upon the Rock

Many years ago, I heard the story about a young boy who went to the beach with his family for their vacation. For weeks, he'd looked forward to playing at the water's edge and building sand castles. On the first day, he made a beautiful castle. It was about two feet tall, and he topped it off with a small red flag to celebrate the completion of his proud construction project. A short time afterward, several older boys, the bully type, happened by. Seeing a much smaller and younger boy gleaming over his castle as others adored his handiwork, one of the bullies simply could not resist the temptation. He walked up to the sand castle, and with a mighty kick which sent sand flying everywhere, the little boy's sand castle was no more!

The same thing happened the following day. On the third day, the little boy determined to make an even bigger, more beautiful castle than ever. This time, he got an idea. He heaved and rolled a heavy rock down to the place where he would build his castle. He worked feverishly on his project. It was his best work yet. At the very center of the structure, was the rock he had rolled down from the berm of the beach. His castle was strong, magnificent, and firm. Sure enough, not long afterward, the gang of bullies came sauntering down the beach, taunting and teasing younger kids and being rude to adults as they went. Finally they came to where the sand castle was. It was the biggest one they had seen him build. It was beautiful. The red flag on its pinnacle swayed back and forth in the brisk breeze from the ocean. How could the leader of the pack of bullies resist the urge to send all that sand flying? The big bully eased back, raised his big foot, and gave the castle a mighty big kick!!! This time, the sand didn't go flying everywhere or anywhere! Instead, the bully let out a horrifying yell, grabbed his big foot up in his hand, and had to be carried away limping by his fellow bullies. I can, with much confidence, imagine now that most readers are smiling, if not laughing out loud, and nodding their heads approvingly at this point. So, what was different about this particular sand castle?

This young boy's third castle was built to last. He designed it to withstand the brutal forces that were sure to come up against it. He knew that his adversary would come sauntering down the beach and would seek to ruin his project. Most importantly, he knew that if he built his castle on a firm foundation such as a rock, it would be devastating for anyone who tried to knock it down. In like manner, Jesus knew that Satan would seek to destroy the Church. To prevent the possibility of catastrophic damage or destruction to the Church, Jesus wisely built it upon Himself. In other words, the kingdom of God is centered in Jesus Christ. This divine decision guarantees that the Church will triumph, regardless of what Satan throws against it.

In Ephesians 1:22-23, the apostle Paul asserts the headship of Jesus over the Church. Not only is He sovereign over creation, but also over the Church. According to the text, Christ was appointed Head of the Church by God the Father. This is rather significant in that this arrangement makes Jesus the Head of the body. No wonder then, that in Matthew 16:18, Jesus asserts that "upon this rock I will build MY church" (emphasis supplied). I doubt that Jesus could have used a stronger possessive term to describe His relation to the Church. In other words, He reigns in, over, and through the Church!

The fact of Christ's headship of the Church lends itself to our better understanding of how we should relate to the Church. Christ's headship should cause us to think carefully about how we relate to the Church, the people of God. It is Christ's Church, not ours. We "ARE" the Church, the body of Christ. We don't own the Church!

A correct theology of the Church impacts positively upon relationships in the Church. Many churches are in varying stages of disarray and decay, because they have not embraced a biblical theology of the Church. There people who believe that the Church revolves around them. They think that they own the Church!

God Is a Strong Tower Around His Church

In His infamous prayer recorded in John 17, Jesus mentioned something rather interesting and important. In vs. 6, He said "I have manifested Your name to the men whom You have given Me out of the world. They were Yours, You gave them to Me, and they have kept Your word." Similarly, in vs. 11, "Now I am no longer in the world, but these are in the world, and I come to You. Holy Father, keep through Your name those whom You have given Me, that they may be one as We are." Finally, in vs. 12, He prayed that "While I was with them in the world, I kept them in Your name. Those whom You gave Me I have kept; and none of them is lost except the son of perdition, that the Scripture might be fulfilled."

What intrigues me about these references to the name of God, is that elsewhere in Scripture, in the book of Proverbs, the name of God is used in a manner that depicts His commitment to protect His people: Proverbs 18:10 – "The name of the LORD is a strong tower: the righteous runs into it, and is safe." In vs. 11, the security and confidence of the rich man is contrasted with the righteous man, "A rich man's wealth is his strong city, and like a high wall in his imagination." On the mount, when Moses asked Him to show him His glory, God proclaimed His name in Exodus 34:5-7, showing Moses His attributes that are most certainly in favor of His people:

> Now the Lord descended in the cloud and stood with him there, and proclaimed the name of the Lord. And the Lord passed before him and proclaimed, "The Lord, the Lord God, merciful and gracious, longsuffering, and abounding in goodness and truth, keeping mercy for thousands, forgiving iniquity and transgression and sin, by no means clearing *the guilty,* visiting the iniquity of the fathers upon the children and the children's children to the third and the fourth generation."

It is reassuring to know that God is merciful and forgiving. When relationships are damaged, it is important to remember that turning to God as our strong tower restores the unity of the church.

Jesus was quite passionate about the unity of the church when He was on earth. He is just as passionate about the unity of the church today while He intercedes for His people before the heavenly throne. He declared that by showing love to one another, the members of the church would establish and maintain their authenticity as His true followers (John 13:34, 35). Jesus prayed for His followers to be one, so the world would believe in Him. Sande argues that unity is an essential part of Christian witness that essentially makes Jesus look good in the eyes of unbelievers when they see His peace operating in the hearts of His followers. A peaceful church is a powerful witness.[1]

Through His apostles, Jesus makes many appeals to His followers to live in harmonious relationship with one another. This is a recurring theme throughout the New Testament. I read several works during the course of my doctoral research in which the writers argue that conflict is necessary. Several scholars proposed that some conflict is good for the church. I will examine a few of these positions later in this book, but suffice it to say that based upon what I have read and studied in the Scriptures, I must stoutly disagree with those learned scholars. A better proposition is that opportunities for growth can arise out of the devastation of conflict.

Conflict is a direct consequence of sin. Disharmony and stress are major manifestations of conflict. That being true, one can reason that it would not be God's will for there to be conflict in the church. Maybe I do know the cause of this reasoning. It could well be that it is the particular definition of a writer, or lack of a universally accepted definition, that fuels this idea of conflict being necessary. It is my position that while disagreements and misunderstandings are inevitable, I do not accept the view that these are the same as conflict. Misunderstanding and disagreement, if handled properly, need not become conflict. It appears somewhat inconsistent to me that some conflict would be "necessary" in a congregation, while Scripture teaches plainly that God is not the author of confusion and division. It is probably more accurate to say that because of the condition of the human heart, there will be conflict in the church. I hold that disagreements are inevitable, but conflict is a choice. Jesus prayed that His followers would be united and loving, and that the unity and peace in the church would be the most powerful witness to unbelievers.

The Church is never one person, but a body of people. Therefore, relationships are implied in this arrangement. This is why love is the foundational principle upon which the Church is built (1 Cor. 13). In Ephesians 5:22-32, Paul speaks of the intimate relationship between Christ and the Church, His people. This loving relationship should be exhibited among His people as well. This was His burden in the Supper Room in John 13 (see Vs. 34, 35).

Jesus was truly concerned about the church. He intended us, the Church, to be His representative agency in the earth. He prayed that the Church should be one, unified (John 17:20-26). Love is the glue that holds the church together (John 13:34, 35). When the church has tough decisions to make, it is this love, not our teachings, not our ministries, not our choir, not the worship style, not our stewardship program that holds us together! "Upon this Rock," is the true source of our unity. It is only as we are individually yoked up with Jesus, and committed to the ideals of what that special relationship looks like, that we can experience success in being the Church Jesus envisioned.

Because God Said So

One of the most amazing realizations that I came to several years ago as I pondered and examined the Church, both from my personal experience as well as a Scriptural perspective, is that for a very long time, Christians and church leaders appear to have erred in making a certain assumption that is all but guaranteed to permit preventable conflict to continue to unnecessarily damage congregations. The assumption that most church people appear to make is that: WHEREAS, people in the church are Christians, and; WHEREAS, Christians love God, and therefore love each other, and; WHEREAS, people who are Christians love each other and love God and should not hurt others; it must THEREFORE be true that, based upon this inherent love, Christians instinctively know how to be the Church Christ envisioned.

Needless to say, this logic is totally flawed! Perhaps you have never actually sat down and intellectually organized your thoughts about the Church in this particular manner, and thus may be shocked that your own assumptions may be at least somewhat similar to the conclusion drawn in the above flawed logic. However, there is strong enough evidence to suggest that there is an urgent need to examine the important question of what makes the Church the Church. What are the biblical principles or distinguishing features that make it different from any other entity in the world?

I would offer that the answer lies in the very meaning of the word "church" which, in the Greek, means "called out." Peter declared that the Church constitutes those who have been "called out of darkness into marvelous light" 1 Peter 2:9, 10. In His prayer for the Church in John 17, Jesus indicated that God had taken the disciples (and all who would believe on Him through their testimony) out of the world in a unique kind of way, in that while we are still "in" the world literally, we are no longer "of" the world morally and spiritually. It seems fitting then, to view the "world" and "darkness" as synonymous. Both terms depict a state of not being in fellowship with God, by not being in a relationship, or not having a connection with Jesus Christ.

John said that Jesus was the light of all mankind (John 1:4-9). Not having a connection with the Light of the world invariably leaves one in darkness. A person is in the world if he is not in Christ, and not in the Church, which is the body of Christ. A person who has not accepted Christ Jesus as his personal Savior and Lord is one who has not chosen to subject himself to the sovereign Lordship and headship of Jesus. Jesus is the Head of the Church, its Protector, Sustainer, and Guide. The Church will be alright... because God said so!

The Church can only be the Church when the headship of Jesus Christ is recognized and demonstrated in the lives of Christians.

This means the members of the church will live in humble submission to Jesus. Proper deference will be shown Him, as the One upon Whom the Church is built and not man. All self-glory and power mongering will be put away from among the followers of Christ, just like it happened among the early disciples once they saw the error of their ways and repented in the upper room in Acts 1.

The Church is a community of believers. No one person is the Church. The Church does not belong to the pastor, elder, deacon, or some politically or financially influential member. It is the Church of the Living God. This fact provides an important assurance, that because the Church is built upon Christ; the gates of hell shall not prevail against it! This was the declaration of Jesus in Matthew 16.

Jesus gives us the assurance that the Church will triumph over Satan's ploys and schemes to destroy her. This assurance can only be made effectual, however, if we, the Church, take our part seriously in adhering to biblical principles that make the Church the Church. Church leaders need to invest more time and resources in teaching, training, and equipping the people of God to live in godly relationship with each other. This type of living is not instinctive, it is instructive. In the same manner that two Christians would fare better if given pre-marital counseling prior to their big day, so too would church members and our relationships if we did not take it for granted that Christians should instinctively know how to live in community with each other.

A biblical understanding of what causes and constitutes conflict, as well as a biblical understanding of how God wants His people to resolve conflict is essential to the peace and prosperity of the Church. Theologically speaking, the majority of conflicts in churches are caused by too much emphasis on self. The biblical commands and instruction on how to address conflict are in some ways uncomfortable for all human beings. However, these instructions are not optional if God's will is to be done, especially among those who are Christians.

Biblical living is the call of the Church. Submission to God is our calling, and even to His Church. No member of the body is a law unto himself. Godly relationships matter, because they rightly represent Christ. That's what He said in John 13:34, 35.

Group Activities

1. Identify and discuss three "assumptions" that negatively (or have the potential to) affect members' understanding of the Church and hinder the growth of our relationship with each other.

2. Make a list of biblical principles that set the parameters for what the Church should look like and be like. Choose a spokesperson to share your findings with the larger group.

3. Choose a partner for this exercise: Now imagine that you are the pastor, head elder, or an officer of "Church of the Solid Rock Which is Jesus Christ" (hopefully, there's no actual church with that name. If there is one either at the time of writing or hereafter, reference to same is purely coincidental on my part). There are some serious issues of conflict plaguing your congregation. You feel led of God to intervene in the crisis by sharing with the congregation that the Church is God's possession, founded upon Christ, and headed by Christ. Develop a one page outline for your presentation. Share your presentation with your partner. Discuss your theological approach. What flaws and strengths did you find as you talked about your presentation?

Reflection Question

1. Write a two page reflection paper that discusses the headship of Jesus Christ, as it relates to light and darkness as
   discussed in this chapter. How does headship theology as
   discussed here inform and contribute to what the Church
   looks like relationally?

Notes

1. Ken Sande, *The Peace Maker: A Biblical Guide to Resolving Personal
   Conflict* (Grand Rapids, MI: Baker Books, 2004), 47-50.

PART TWO

FACING THE MONSTER OF CHURCH CONFLICT

CHAPTER 4

If We Can't Even Agree on That!

There are many characterizations or definitions of conflict in the literature that speaks to the field of conflict ministry. What appears consistent in the literature is that there is no definite or conclusive agreement concerning what conflict is. In other words, there are many conflicting views of what constitutes conflict! Some of these characterizations of conflict include: Bullard, who holds that "simply defined, conflict is the struggle of two objects seeking to occupy the same space at the same time."[1] Poirier argues that rather than being intrusions into ministry, conflicts are instead "assignments from God—the very means by which he causes us to see our poverty and the riches of his wisdom, power, justice, and mercy."[2] Stagner refers to conflict as "a situation in which two or more human beings desire goals which they perceive as being attainable by one or the other but not by both."[3] Speed B. Leas reasoned that the inability of getting a definitive grasp on what constitutes conflict may be found in the fact that "we use one word – conflict - to describe many different experiences and situations, but each of the experiences so named are not all the same."[4]

I happen to agree with Leas, in that the term conflict is probably too loosely used. It is my view that some normal disagreements are unnecessarily referred to as conflict, and that some major conflicts are minimized and referred to as normal or even healthy conflict. Clearly then, there may be an opportunity here for more intentional work to seek an industry-wide consensus on what constitutes conflict. I acknowledge that this is a tall order, but I view this as an important factor in seeking to develop more consistent approaches to conflict resolution. Currently, the literature in the field of conflict resolution appears to be struggling with of one of the main problems with conflict—the lack of a universally accepted consensus on a working definition of conflict.

Other contributors' characterizations of conflict include: Sande, who views conflict as "a difference in opinion or purpose that frustrates someone's goals or desires."[5] Van Yperen holds that "church conflict is always theological, never merely inter-personal... is always about leadership, character, and community."[6] Mayer makes a good point, when he posits that "conflict emerges and is experienced along cognitive (perceptive), emotional (feeling), and behavioral (action) dimensions."[7] This characterization appears more complete than the usual focus on behavior only, rendering the issues rather limited. This limitation would undoubtedly also restrict the range of optional approaches utilized, in order to successfully intervene in the given matter.

Ramsbotham, Woodhouse, and Miall view conflict as "the pursuit of incompatible goals by different groups."[8] This is a good example of over-simplification, from my perspective. I have seen how this view in and of itself has sparked conflict. This rather loose characterization does not take into account the right of individuals to freely express differing viewpoints, without being accused of harm or offense to others. It seems to me that incompatible goals, in and of themselves, should not be seen as conflict. However, poor handling of those differences can become conflicted.

This, again, is an area where more work could be done in the conflict ministry field to come to consensus on the meaning of conflict. Perhaps a good illustration of this concern can be seen in what Lederach points out in his work on conflict transformation. On a visit to Central America in the 1980s, he found that the term "conflict resolution" was viewed with suspicion by the natives, who during those times of socio-political unrest across the region, perceived the term as an attempt to stifle genuine disagreement and necessary advocacy. They felt that the goal or emphasis of conflict resolution was one way to deny needed changes, in other words, to muzzle them. This caused Lederach to realize that people's perceptions of terminologies, and the meanings attached to them, may be a source of conditions that can indeed escalate conflict.[9]

Certainly, more could be said about the many characterizations or definitions of conflict, but suffice it to say that I have presented a good sampling here of the complexities involved in agreeing to what congregations are wrestling with—conflict that must first be defined, then acknowledged, and then properly concluded. It is only fitting that having come to the realization that there are many variations of the definition of conflict in the field of conflict resolution theory and practice; I should propose a working definition that would be congruent with this need for definition.

I therefore offer that conflict is a state of tension or alienation between two or more parties, resulting from malice (desire or action to inflict harm, injury or suffering upon another) or the mishandling of a disagreement. If we can't agree on a definition of conflict, I rather doubt that our best efforts to resolve many conflict situations will be successful. I will now turn attention to what various conflict resolution theorists and experts deem to be the causes of congregational conflict.

Group Activities

1. Compare and contrast at least five author's definition of conflict referenced in this chapter. What are the pros and cons of those you have chosen?

2. Seek to coin a definition of conflict as a group, and compare your definition with other groups' responses.

3. As a group, discuss how understanding and perceptions of the word conflict can lead to conflict or resolve conflict. Give specific examples of positive and negative results.

Reflection

1. Write a one paragraph personal reflection on a past conflict that you had with a church member. Describe in your paragraph how you felt when you realized that you had an entirely different understanding of what conflict is. Talk about how you felt when the conflict dragged on because your definitions of conflict were not similar.

2. On your paper, also write down your thoughts concerning what you would do different if the same dispute occurred today.

3. Write your thoughts about the principles that have impacted you so far in this book. Be sure to also reflect on your local church setting, both past and present. How could certain serious church problems have been minimized or avoided in the past? How do you feel about your personal readiness to provide conflict ministry now that you have been exposed to the principles in this book?

Notes

1. George W. Bullard Jr., *Every Congregation Needs a Little Conflict* (St. Louis, MO: Chalice Press, 2008), 10.

2. Alfred Poirier, *The Peace Making Pastor: A Biblical Guide to Resolving Church Conflict* (Grand Rapids, MI: Baker Books, 2006), 14.

3. Ross Stagner, comp., "The Dimensions of Human Conflict" (Detroit, MI: Wayne State University Press, 1967), 136, quoted in McSwain and Treadwell, *Conflict Ministry in the Church*, 17.

4. Speed B. Leas, introduction to *Conflict Management in Congregations*, edited by David B. Lott (Herndon, VA: The Alban Institute, 2001), 4.

5. Sande, *The Peace Maker*, 29.

6. Van Yperen, *Making Peace,* 24.

7. Bernard Mayer, *The Dynamics of Conflict: A Guide to Engagement and Intervention* (San Francisco: Josey-Bass, 2012), 4.

8. Oliver Ramsbotham, Tom Woodhouse, and Hugh Miall, *Contemporary Conflict Resolution* (Malden, MA: Polity Press, 2011), 30.

9. John Paul Lederach, *The Little Book of Conflict Transformation* (Intercourse, PA: Good Books, 2003), 3.

CHAPTER 5

Getting to the Heart of the Matter

At the time of this writing, I have lived in three countries and been a member of several local churches. I have seen a lot of conflict in churches. As a lay member, I witnessed my pastors being unfairly treated sometimes. I have seen pastors being slandered, with no way to defend themselves or to protect their wives and children from the wrath of unmerciful church members. Sometimes, I have seen where the pastor perhaps could have done some things differently in terms of his approach or method, but never to the extent that merited, deserved, or justified being abused.

As a pastor myself, I have been abused by clergy killers in two congregations where I have served in the past. In the first case, my abuser was a man. In the second case, it was both a woman and a man. In every case, whether it was a matter of abuse or other manifestations of conflict, my style has been to seek to understand how and why things escalated to where conflict occurred. In the case of the woman mentioned above, I am known to share in my seminars that "I've pastored Jezebel!" I know this may appear somewhat graceless, but if you knew the details, you would likely agree.

This was a case where a certain female member in a church was the reigning "queen" or "owner" of the church when I arrived. I say "owner" because she claimed and was apparently convinced that "this is 'our' church (possessive usage)." She practically ran the church. She was strong-willed, rude, disrespectful, overbearing, and rich. Her husband was a highly paid professional who hardly said a word. It was the opinion of most that she wore the pants. She intimidated the members, including the men of the church. We were bound to have a showdown sooner or later. It was sooner.

Several attempts on my part to meet with her to resolve the problems she had caused by inviting an unauthorized person to preach (she herself did not have the authority to issue such invitations) met with absolutely no response. I resorted to canceling the occasion and disinvited the speaker. She decided, like Jezebel, that her mission from that point forward would be to destroy me and ruin my ministry. You would not believe the things she said about me in several emails that she sent to the entire membership, plus non-members, over the course of several months after that. It is this blatant attack on my reputation and character, and her clear intention to destroy my ministry and hurt my family that makes her Jezebel.

My family members were savagely attacked with the most vitriolic slander I have ever witnessed in any church or among those who claim to be followers of Jesus. It was devastating. Members of our attacker's large clan sided with her, along with several other non-related members. This was amazing, given that her conduct was clearly un-Christlike. Her husband validated the views other church members had concerning his fear of his wife. Not only did he remain completely silent in the midst of her abusive campaign against me, my family members, and against any member (including the head elder) who dared to express support for me or concerns about her conduct, but he surprised everyone when he suddenly "found his voice" to express support for her cruel behavior (some mockingly suggested that he probably couldn't go home if he didn't). On a more serious note, it should be stated that this brother did not have a reputation for any kind of unchristian attitude or conduct. This poor man felt obliged to defend the indefensible behavior of a family member, perhaps because of his own embarrassment.

Greenfield argues that clergy killers and pathological antagonists are responsible for the abuse of ministers in many local churches. He argues that these are usually people who have some form of personality disorder, or are simply just evil.[1] His work is perhaps the most self-effacing description of a pastor's journey in ministry that I have ever encountered. To be sure, not all conflicts fall into the category of the worst kind of intentional destruction that Greenfield sets forth, but personality disorders constitute a realistic contributor to conflict in every context of life. Sometimes, the possibility of personality disorders are not factored into congregational conflict.

This lack of attribution may be due to ignorance or naiveté on the part of church leaders and members. There are psychologically challenged people in every aspect of life, including congregational life, who abuse others. In their work on the effects of personality disorders in the workplace, Cavaiola and Lavender examine the typical issues caused by individuals who are affected by the various disorders, such as: narcissism, histrionic personality, antisocial personality, borderline personality disorder, obsessive compulsive personality, dependent personality disorder, passive aggressive personality, avoidant personality, schizophrenia, and paranoid personality. I will not go into an examination of these respective disorders, as such scientific analysis is outside the scope of this book.

The astute church leader, student, or church member would benefit greatly from a working knowledge of these personality disorders in order to better understand how people respond and react to stress, and be better able to manage conflict or potential conflict situations that may arise. Cavaiola and Lavender define personality disorders as follows:

> Personality disorders are long-standing disturbances in personality that usually begin in late adolescence and continue throughout adulthood. They reveal themselves when an individual engages in repetitive patterns of nonproductive interactions with others, which is a manifestation of the impaired aspects of their personality. Personality disorders cause a person to consistently act in disturbing patterns of behavior in both occupational and social relationships . . . an individual can have traits of several different types of personality disorders; there really is no one "pure" type. Also, personality-disordered people can have different intensities or severity of their disorder.[2]

Most assuredly, whatever affects the workplace, most likely also affects the church. My purpose for including this awareness of personality disorders in the conflict process is not to cast undue negative aspersions upon people affected by these disorders, but rather to heighten awareness of an aspect of conflicted churches that is often overlooked. The conflict minister would be wise to keep this perspective in mind, while recognizing God's power to help those affected by these negative, disordered behavior patterns. I must caution readers against falling into the temptation of judging people, or of making clinical diagnoses about others when it is not within the realm of their legal authority or professional expertise to do so.

Haugk produced a classic work on one aspect of what Cavaiola and Lavender so ably treated in their work cited above. He deals with the damaging effects of antagonists in the church, from the perspective of personality disorders. Again, while the aim of my book is not to attempt an exhaustive treatment of the social or psychological science background of my topic, I hold to the view that at the minimum, church leaders would greatly benefit from at least a basic working knowledge of personality disorder issues as they relate to conflicts in the church. Haugk states that "antagonists are individuals who, on the basis of nonsubstantive [sic] evidence, go out of their way to make insatiable demands, usually attacking the person or performance of others. These attacks are selfish in nature, tearing down rather than building up, and are frequently directed against those in a leadership capacity."[3]

Haugk also asserts that:

> Antagonists frequently evidence at least several of five personality characteristics: negative self-concept, narcissism, aggression, rigidity, and authoritarianism. Although these same personality traits occur in "normal" individuals as well, two factors distinguish these characteristics as they appear in antagonists: first, antagonists usually display at least several of them; second, antagonists exhibit them in extreme forms.[4]

Pneuman identifies nine causes of church conflict: (1) differences in beliefs and values; (2) structural ambiguity; (3) congregants' conflicts with the pastor's role and responsibilities; (4) an outdated congregational structure that no longer fits the congregation's size; (5) conflicting clergy and lay leadership styles, in particular, differences between consultative versus authoritarian styles of leadership; (6) the new pastor making changes too quickly; (7) clogged communication channels as conflict escalates; (8) general mismanagement of conflict by church members; and (9) disaffected members hold back participation and pledges.[5]

While Pneuman makes a compelling case for the causes of conflict, there is one of his points that I would comment on. The sixth cause he gives is not without debate, as it is common knowledge that there will be some church members who will oppose change no matter how or when it is implemented. I concur that changes that are done too quickly may be a trigger for conflict. However, for some people, change at any time and for any reason is deemed a threat, once they have come to regard that which is being changed as a sacred symbol. In my own pastorates, I have found that no amount of tactful and timely communication, no amount of intentional and careful implementation, will prevent some people from claiming that the change was too sudden, unnecessary, or that they were unaware of the pending change. They will accuse the change agent, usually their pastor, of being inconsiderate, simply because they feel as if they are "losing" something personal in the process.

Sande and Johnson posit that "conflict happens when you are at odds with another person over what you think, want, or do."[6] Sometimes, Pneuman's sixth cause of conflict is the very essence of what Sande and Johnson claim. They (Sande and Johnson) further explain that other factors also contribute to the start of conflict: God-given diversity; simple misunderstandings; sinful attitudes and desires; and sinful human nature.[7]

Poirier, in his discourse on the heart of conflict, addresses such causes similar to those espoused by Sande and Johnson. Elaborating on James 4:1-5:6, he discusses various kinds of desires as primary causes of conflict, and the inter-personal damage they produce in relationships. However, Poirier adds that "the real problem is not simply that we have broken relationship with others. We have broken relationship with God. Our sinful conflicts reveal and reflect our broken relationship with God."[8]

Van Yperen deals with the root causes of conflict in a most pointed and enlightening manner. He cites cultural issues such as the Western pre-occupation with individual needs, the chronic self-help mentality, the "what's in it for me?" mindset, and consumerism as major problems that undermine the Christo-centric appeal of the gospel. He further shows that structural issues contribute to conflict. By structure, he means the system of the organizational (local church or denominational) structure, and with reference to how these systems impact the decision-making process. Often, the "way" things are done, serves as a catalyst for conflict. In this regard, Van Yperen correctly asserts that not all conflict is personal, as indeed, much conflict can be shown to be systemic (structure based) in nature. This viewpoint therefore represents the need to accurately get to the source of conflict, rather than merely treating the symptoms with well-intentioned remedies that may not speak in a relevant and successful manner to the actual underlying issues – the heart of the matter.

Spiritual issues, such as putting oneself first, failing to confess or repent of sins (while claiming to be forgiven or even demanding forgiveness from the offended), and of failing to be holy through transformation within the context of Christian community, all significantly contribute to the potential for church conflict. The renewed heart of the members is critical in order that the church can be what God ordained it to be. Van Yperen makes the bold claim that "all church conflict is theological." This speaks to his view that the church has become a theologically faulty, autonomous entity, rather than an entity which operates on the basis of spiritual integrity. In this, he posits the thought-provoking view that integrity, from the word "integer" which means *whole* or *complete* or something undivided, is the calling of the church; not autonomy, which means *self-ruling* and *independent*.[9]

Of particular concern to me is the problem of autonomy. Out of this mindset flow most of the ills of congregational dysfunction here-to-fore described. I have witnessed first-hand the damaging consequences of autonomous attitudes that inspire some members to develop the belief that "this is our church!" Clearly, this is a cause of serious conflict in many places, given that pastors are then rendered incapable of moving the church forward, if in fact, those with an autonomous viewpoint do not see eye-to-eye with the pastor's vision and direction. The theological reality is that the church is God's church, and that all the members together (the integer, the undivided whole) make up the body of Christ, the church. The church belongs to no one but God alone, and is not the property of humans. This theologically incorrect mindset is a primary source of major church conflict in many places and results in power struggles between laity and clergy.

The attitude that "this is our church" obviously fails to take into account the fact that the pastor is also a member of the community of believers. In his contribution to better equip the pastor, Staples answers the question "What is the church?" He gives vital insight into the pastor's role as a member of the church community — one who works to build the community.[10] Obviously, a faith community or local church that sees their pastor as not belonging to the community, as they would view an outsider, will not be quick to trust or follow their pastor. A biblical understanding of what and who constitutes the church, and what is God's purpose for the church is vital in insuring healthy attitudes and better capability for avoiding preventable conflicts.

A pastor who is viewed as an outsider will be treated like an intruder whenever he or she tries to lead. While it is true that taking time to know the members will alleviate some of the potential distance between pastor and congregation, the simple fact is that there will always be a perhaps small, but significantly influential group who will never readily relinquish their hold on a church. They are driven by the need to seize and hoard power. The pastor is then viewed as a threat to their power in "their church."

Much more could be said about the causes of church conflict. The main idea here however, is to establish that conflict is perhaps not as simple or simplistic as oftentimes perceived. Many Christians are weary of conceding the fact of conflict's presence among them, simply because it feels out of place for Christians to be at odds. At the same time though, this denial often provides the context for more conflict. As minor issues are left unresolved, opportunities for learning how to resolve minor conflict are lost. Minor issues grow into damaging conflict that leads to dysfunction in the church.

Of note too, is the reality that there is great complexity surrounding how conflict starts and develops. Nevertheless, the power of the Cross, rightly understood and applied to the life of those who have been transformed by the gospel of Christ, is the power behind the ministry of reconciliation.

Group Discussion

1. Get into groups of 3-4. Discuss what you would do if you wanted to initiate a different order of service (liturgy). Be sure to include ideas about the change process as found in at least one writer's work (cite reference).

2. Discuss at least five personality disorders. How would you seek to address members who are affected by these disorders, if you found yourself in a conflict situation with them?

3. What steps should be taken to get to the root cause of a conflict (write down your steps, with a brief explanation of each).

4. Discuss the causes of congregational conflict and offer possible remedies for each.

Reflection Questions

1. How do you respond or react to conflict or the threat of conflict? Are you aware of your conflict style? Write a private note to yourself about how you typically relate to conflict. Then answer this question: how can I do a better job of managing how I deal with conflict?

2. You are being attacked by a member of your congregation, and the abuse if hurting not only you, your ministry, but also your spouse and children. What would you do to resolve the broken relationship and stop the abuse?

3. Journal your reactions and responses, including your inner feelings for the next fourteen days, chronicling every conflict or threat of conflict that you have with your spouse, family member, coworker, supervisor, stranger, etc. At the end of the journaling period, review and compare how you have felt or reacted to various types of conflict. What are your findings about yourself? In what ways do you think you can grow in how you respond to conflict situations? Write your answers in your journal. This is a private exercise just for you.

Notes

1. Guy Greenfield, *The Wounded Minister: Healing From and Preventing Personal Attacks* (Grand Rapids, MI: Baker Book House, 2001), 25.

2. Alan A. Cavaiola and Neil J. Lavender, *Toxic Coworkers: How to Deal with Dysfunctional People on the Job; Working with Narcissists, Borderlines, Sociopaths, Schizoids, and Others* (Oakland, CA: New Harbinger Publications, 2000), 4.

3. Kenneth C. Haugk, *Antagonists in the Church: How to Identify and Deal with Destructive Conflict* (Minneapolis, MN: Augsburg Publishing House, 1988), 59.

4. Ibid., 60-61.

5. Roy W. Pneuman, "Nine Common Sources of Conflict in Congregations," in *Conflict Management in Congregations,* ed. David B. Lott (Herndon, VA: The Alban Institute, 2001), 45-53.

6. Ken Sande and Kevin Johnson, *Resolving Everyday Conflict* (Grand Rapids, MI: Baker Books, 2011), 14.

7. Ibid., 16-19.

8. Poirier, *The Peace Making Pastor,* 50-59.

9. Van Yperen, *Making Peace,* 27-46.

10. Russell L. Staples, "The Minister as a Member of the Community," in *The Adventist Minister,* ed. C. Raymond Holmes and Douglas Kilcher (Berrien Springs, MI: Andrews University Press, 1991), 45-52.

CHAPTER 6

Good, Bad, or Just Plain ol' Ugly?

I have conducted hundreds of church board and church business meetings. As a rule, I do not tolerate any conduct that hurts people in the meetings that I chair. I lay down ground rules, such as verbally informing members that every participant in meetings is personally responsible for his or her words, actions and attitudes, and that I am not authorized by God to allow any person to hurt another in these meetings. During the first meeting of every new term of office, I have the board to vote a Church Board Code of Conduct document that outlines the expectations and responsibilities enjoined upon board members. My job and responsibility is to conduct meetings with professionalism, seeing to it that every participant is able to freely and respectfully contribute to the proceedings, and to insure that at the end of the meeting, each member's dignity is intact. The members of the churches where I have pastored can attest that I have insisted on this protocol in my pastoral guardianship of the church.

There have been times when individuals have stepped out of line and violated the Code of Conduct, causing hurt to others, including me. They did not get off lightly. Leadership is a key component in congregational transformation. Leadership requires tremendous courage and fortitude. Leading change in conflicted churches is especially challenging, but God has promised His servants His power to accomplish His will.

What is your conception of conflict? Is conflict good, bad, or just plain ol' ugly? This is an important question. Our conception of conflict determines how we relate to others and what kind of attitude we manifest when there is conflict. It is also important to note that our conception determines if we cause conflict. One party may view a dispute as conflict, but the other party may only regard it as a disagreement. Both parties are involved in the same situation, but see it from different perspectives. Unless and until they both clarify their conceptions or perspectives, it is unlikely that the dispute will be properly concluded. Not only that, but it is very likely that the matter will deteriorate further into conflict.

I have read widely in the area of congregational conflict resolution. There are writers who suggest that conflict is necessary. Others hold that it is a moral issue, and does not fit into the will of God. A few appear to be undecided about whether conflict is good or bad, choosing rather to focus on how to resolve or otherwise conclude conflict. As in the secular context, some religious authors have suggested the idea of conflict management. The question before us in this section is whether conflict is necessary, moral, or even unavoidable.

My position is that disagreement is normal, natural, healthy and needed in any relationship or organization. Though disagreement is normal and natural and should be both expected and welcome even in the church, it is my view that conflict is a choice. My determined purpose in life is to show that disagreement is not license to cause conflict. Disagreement is not conflict. Careless disregard for the views of others or for their right to preserve their personal dignity is often the cause of conflict. People choose to act and speak in ways that result in conflict.

If an individual regards aggressive, reckless, uncouth speech and offensive attitudes as an acceptable way to communicate, he may feel that the person he offends by his uncultured manners is someone who needs to grow some skin. Further, he may rationalize that his behavior was not offensive, but that the dispute they had was a mere disagreement. I see this rationalization of wrong-doing a lot in my work. Rude, uncouth people who habitually offend and cause hurt to others are not as quick to concede that they have caused conflict. They pass it off as a "disagreement" that the offended party should accept as merely that, and get over it. They have no remorse about their behavior. On the other hand, someone is left to nurse bruised feelings and devastated dignity. This discussion focuses the spotlight on the relationship between conception and consequences.

Goertzen, in referencing several studies that indicate the severe lack of conflict management knowledge and expertise, states that "such statistics, alarming as they are, indicate the need for conflict management, but also simply reflect the obvious; the Church in general and Christians in particular are not immune to conflict."[1] Not only is the church not immune to conflict, but the church is often guilty of accommodating, even protecting people who cause conflict. Haugk argues that "for too long, congregations have been places where antagonists can operate with success."[2]

This reality exists because: (1) many Christians are instinctively repulsed by the word "conflict" and therefore cringe to acknowledge its existence among them; and (2) many Christians are instinctively repulsed by the suggestion of any form of church discipline, even against clearly seen wrong-doers who are damaging the church. At the same time, however, the conflict continues to grow, and even though most members will not personally get involved to help find constructive ways to resolve the problems, they almost always blame church leadership for the horrible damage that results from inaction.

One of the most frustrating realities for church leaders is the challenge of knowing that conflict is working like leaven throughout the congregation, yet most well-intentioned members are unwilling or feel unable to constructively participate in the resolution process. This may be due either to crippling fear or misconceptions about conflict. Bixby observes that "we may never be able to rid ourselves of conflict altogether, but we can contain it and limit its power."[3] This sentiment, viewed against the backdrop of the many and varied types of problems inherent in church structures, shows the need for intentional education of congregations on conflict ministry and the ministry of reconciliation. Goertzen speaks to the inevitability of church conflict, reasoning that there are theological, sociological, and psychological reasons why this is so.[4]

A young pastor once told me that a senior minister gave him some "good advice," that "if you love the people, you won't have any problems with them." Not only was I shocked, I was mortified! While I am certain that this senior pastor meant well, his advice speaks to one of the conceptions (in this case, misconceptions) people, including church leaders, have about congregational conflict. Jesus, Moses, and Nehemiah all dearly loved the people whom they served, but that fact certainly did not exempt them from being attacked, ill-treated, slandered, and hated. Jesus was eventually killed by the very ones he came to save, heal, and forgive. De Ville aptly makes this point in his work.[5]

The general conception of conflict as a negative, bad or un-Christlike reality to be denied or passively ignored is extremely unhealthy for the church. To deny or ignore the obvious presence of church conflict is both self-deceptive and dangerous. This is not to say that conflict should be welcome or encouraged. However, it is to no one's advantage that its presence be ignored and left untreated, no more than is cancer. The typical conception of conflict among most church members is that conflict is evil, and therefore is best denied, is best swept under the proverbial rug, or simply prayed about. This may be partly due to the church's sometimes unbalanced emphasis on peace, harmony and love. Conflict, by its very nature, is inconsistent with these Christian ideals, hence the typical non-confrontational passivity among most Christians whenever conflict raises its ugly head.

Group Discussion

1. Discuss in your groups whether conflict is good, bad, or just plain ol' ugly.

2. Come up with a suggested Code of Conduct for your church board.

3. Spend some time building on the discussion of conception of conflict and consequences.

4. Most congregational conflict is not resolved in a timely manner, but is swept under the rug. What biblical texts and principles would your group draw upon to explain to a congregation that this is not a healthy or productive way to handle conflict?

Notes

1. Leroy W. Goertzen, *Understanding, Managing & Redeeming Church Conflict* (Lexington, KY: Corban University, 2012), 9-10.

2. Haugk, *Antagonists in the Church,* 39.

3. Douglas J. Bixby, *Challenging the Church Monster: From Conflict to Community* (Eugene, OR: Wipf and Stock Publishers, 2007), 17.

4. Goertzen, *Understanding, Managing & Redeeming,* 23-40.

5. Jard De Ville, *The Pastor's Handbook of Interpersonal Relationships: Keys to Successful Leadership* (Silver Spring, MD: Review and Herald Graphics, 1995), 129-133.

CHAPTER 7

Stately Steeples and Steaming Saints!

A vast amount of money is spent every year in America building awe-inspiring church edifices. However, in so many cities and towns across this great country, most people do not attend anybody's church! With so many churches of every theological persuasion, physical description and membership size, it seems as if there should be many more Christians in the land. Over the last two years, I have lead two different congregations into conducting community surveys to determine what people around us are looking for in a church, as well as to find out what their felt needs were with a view to matching our resources with those needs – my definition of ministry.

The responses to the question of "why do you think so many people do not attend church?" garnered only a few different categories of responses, primarily: (1) "there are too many hypocrites in the church," (2) "church people are too judgmental," and (3) "the churches don't come into the neighborhood like what you are doing to let us know who they are." Unfortunately, the mission of the church to proclaim good news has been undermined by much bad news about the church itself. People are looking at the church and are wondering out loud, "why is there so much conflict in churches?"

Thy ask, "why spend so much money building these beautiful church buildings, while what goes on inside of them among the members and church leaders is oftentimes anything but beautiful?" In fact, many churches actually split and some are completely destroyed, precisely over disagreements and conflict encountered during the building project for their beautiful edifice! "Where is the love of Jesus among church folks?"

The saints are angry. Most of them don't even know why they are angry. Stately steeples and steaming saints is an oxymoron that does not auger well for the preaching of the gospel and the ushering in of Christ's return. The Bible is clear. Nothing of powerful significance will happen in or through the church as long as the members are not on one accord and receive the baptism of the Holy Spirit (Acts 1 and 2). Congregational conflict not only affects the church members, but also the outside community. In-fighting distracts the church from the vital work of disciple-making, and saps the energies of those who would venture to work for Christ. Congregational conflict is a lose-lose proposition. There are no winners. No wonder Jesus declared in John 13:34, 35 that it is the love among the members of His church that will impress and convince the world that we are His disciples. Only then will the world see a good reason to open their ears and hearts to hear what we have to say about a God Who sent His only begotten Son.

There are many kinds of damaging results that can accrue from improperly handled conflict in a local church. It is generally understood that the membership experiences severe stress during times of congregational conflict. The stress in times of severe church conflict situations often results in fight, flight, or freeze responses by the membership. Where isolated individuals are at odds, they are directly affected, but the church is not necessarily exempt from feeling the consequences of their personal fallout. The church's witness and influence in the community may also be negatively impacted as knowledge of the internal problems becomes public. One aspect of consequences arising from conflict that is sometimes overlooked, is the impact conflict has on pastors and their families.

Bolton writes:

> I detest conflict because at best it is disruptive, and at worst it is destructive. Once it erupts, conflict is difficult to control. Destructive controversy has a tendency to expand. Often it becomes detached from its initial causes and may continue after these have become irrelevant or have long been forgotten. Conflict frequently escalates until it consumes all the things and people it touches.[1]

What Bolton here describes is typically what causes the human psyche to activate protective mechanisms to primarily seek an escape from conflict or stress triggered by the threat of conflict. The fear of conflict and its consequences triggers an involuntary physiological reaction commonly known as fight or flight. These commonly recognized adrenaline inspired auto responses serve as a means of survival or escape from perceived threat or danger.

Ursiny concurs with the established view that the fight-flight response is the result of a fear of harm. He explains the role and place of the two responses as follows:

> Human beings have a built in fight-or-flight instinct, and many times the wiser person will take the flight option. It is smart to avoid a dangerous area of a city that you have never been to before. It shows wisdom to get out of a physically abusive relationship. . . . However, sometimes we have a flight response in

reaction to a false perception of harm. In our minds we can exaggerate the emotional harm someone can cause us in a relationship. The more we exaggerate the harm, the more likely it is that we will avoid the conflict. This explains why some people are better able to face conflict with general acquaintances than with loved ones. The more we love and respect someone, the more vulnerable we feel to being emotionally hurt by his or her reaction. On the other hand, facing conflict [fight] is most important to do with those with whom we want intimate relationships. Therefore, we often need to risk getting hurt feelings in order to bring the relationship to a deeper level.[2]

The concept of fight-flight was theorized and popularized by physiologist Dr. Walter Bradford Cannon when he published *The Wisdom of the Body* in 1932.[3] In recent years, another dimension has been added to the flight-fight concept. It is the freeze effect or freeze response. Neuro-scientists have recently been recognizing and giving more attention to this fear or stress response of the brain. A common illustration of this response is the "deer in the headlight" phenomenon. It is regarded as a response of hopelessness or giving up. Barth explains it this way: "Sometimes our brain, in its frozen state, leads us to a sense of helplessness, hopelessness and/or apathy. 'I can't do anything about it, it's too big for me, might as well just accept it', are all reactions to that frozen brain."[4]

This is a developing conversation to watch in the scientific community, as it somewhat revolutionizes the previously held views about stress responses in the brain. Again, this book is not primarily concerned with scientific psychological research, per-se, except to the extent that established facts may be able to answer and clarify some of the questions which impact this subject of conflict ministry.

I decided to explore the outer edges of the flight-fight-freeze concept because of the value it appears to present in understanding some of the consequences of catastrophic church conflict. I proffer that the congregation as a whole reacts in much the same way to catastrophic conflict as do individuals. It is well established in the literature that members either flee or fight during major conflict situations. I will therefore limit any further attention of fight-flight-freeze to the freeze aspect of this stress response.

Congregations sometimes freeze when a significant portion of the members who have not fled get to the place of perceived hopelessness regarding any recovery from the prevailing conflict. This sense of lethargy and apathy takes over the mood of the congregation and the result is stagnation, which I will refer to as "the comatose state," during which period, if the church is not resuscitated through specialized intervention efforts, may eventually result in death. My analysis of the literature, supported by my personal observations of conflicted churches, is that sometimes the actual issue which sparked the conflict in the first place, is not what brings about coma or death. It is instead the freezing of the members as a result of despair, due to any combination of reasons with respect to their inability or unwillingness to effectively deal with conflict. They lose hope. They neither fight nor flee. They merely exist, and continue to go through the motions of church attendance, with no particular missional or relational purpose in mind.

Another aspect of consequences that might accrue from catastrophic church conflict is the diminished witness and influence of the church in the community. It is no secret that church fights tend to become public knowledge outside the church. The evening news has carried stories of local church fights in many towns and cities. People have posted videos of embarrassing church quarrels and physical altercations on popular social sites such as Youtube and

Facebook. Newspaper columnists have expressed alarm and even made fun of distasteful behavior by members of local churches in their cities. Given the reality of instant news and the plethora of amateur pseudo-journalists who are armed with mobile phones and video cameras, but not encumbered with a great deal of regard for the privacy of anyone, church conflicts have and will continue to undermine the effectiveness of the church in this generation.

As disgruntled and hurt members flee conflicted churches, they take with them and spread the stories of horror, sometimes with a dose of exaggeration for good measure. To make matters worse, those who leave tend not to tell the whole truth about what happened. They certainly do not tell how they may have contributed to the conflict. Most church members are ill-equipped or unwilling to properly handle conflict, opting instead to fight, flee, or freeze.

Runde and Flanagan identify and describe five levels of intensity related to conflict situations: level 1 - differences, level 2 - misunderstandings, level 3 - disagreements, level 4 - discord, and level 5 - polarization. It is from level 3-5 that conflict begins to get ugly. These writers note that level 3 (disagreements) "are basically differences with an attitude."[5] Shawchuck says that destructive conflict is cyclical in nature, generating patterns of conduct in persons and organizations that soon become predictable to the skillful observer.[6] The reality of cyclical conflict is a good reason for churches to become educated in conflict ministry. Barthel and Edling argue, "For the sake of Christ's reputation in the world, God calls on his people to do all they can to bring a definite end to conflict."[7]

The toll of congregational conflict on pastors and their families is unimaginable and incalculable. According to Pastoral Care Inc., the number one reason pastors leave the ministry, is that "church people are not willing to go the same direction and goal of the pastor. Pastors believe God wants them to go in one direction but the people are not willing to follow or change."[8] In this same survey, the research team found out the following about pastors:

1. 75% report a significant stress-related crisis at least once in their ministry.

2. 90% of pastors said the ministry was completely different than what they thought it would be like before they entered the ministry.

3. 40% report serious conflict with a parishioner at least once a month.

4. 50% of pastors feel so discouraged that they would leave the ministry if they could, but have no other way of making a living.

5. 50% of the ministers starting out will not last 5 years.

6. 1 out of every 10 ministers will actually retire as a minister in some form.

7. 80% of pastors' spouses wish their spouse would choose a different profession.

8. Over 1,700 pastors left the ministry every month last year.

9. Over 1,300 pastors were terminated by the local church each month, many without cause.[9]

These statistics paint a dismal picture of the realities of pastoral ministry in America today. Pastors and their families, who give so much at great personal sacrifice, are often abused by those to whom they minister. Susek counseled that "leadership today is potentially lethal to a career. Taking biblically correct action does not guarantee a biblically correct response from the board and/or congregation."[10] Susek continues by illustrating how deep-rooted and unsolved conflict in churches often resulted in the congregation being "focused on superficial problems instead" and abusing their pastors, seeing they seem able to find unity in that particular activity.[11]

A quarter of a century ago, Haugk wrote that "recent literature in the area of conflict resolution has begun to recognize that there are individuals who initiate and thrive on unhealthy conflict, persons who have no desire whatsoever to see conflict resolved."[12] Unfortunately for the pastor, antagonists concentrate their mischief on church leaders, the authority figure in the church. The statistics show that there is a real human toll being paid in broken lives of abused clergy and their families. Pastors' children leave the church in alarming numbers. No longer do the sons of the prophets flock to the schools of the prophets to be trained for the ministry, for they have seen too much. Ministry leads change. Change breeds conflict.

Nelson and Appel wrote that "leaders need to realize that not all of the conflict that the improvement plan can manifest is created by the change itself."[13] This view was expressed against the backdrop of the assumption that the conflicts normally surrounding transitions initiated by pastors is always because of something that the pastor did wrong in the change process. The writers show here that oftentimes "people are prone to transfer their anger and frustrations onto moving objects. They attach their baggage to current affairs, even though they may be totally unrelated."[14]

Catastrophic conflict has serious as well as long-term consequences for churches, communities, and also for clergy and their families. Fight-flight-freeze has impacted many churches, leaving a terrible trail of wounded church members. Communities have been denied their right to see the faithful witness of Christ exemplified by the loving, united relationships among professed Christians. Many pastors and their families have been badly and even permanently damaged by cruel abusers and ill-formed organizational structures that weakened or ruined their ministry.

There is no wonder then, that so many pastors are forced out of the ministry every year, largely because of church members' resistance to the changes they propose. All human beings struggle with change, and all must wrestle with the complex emotions surrounding transitions. From appearances, it appears that most people react to change in negative ways. Unfortunately, in the church, anger and frustration are normally directed against the visible agent and advocate of change—the pastor. The aftermath is often devastating.

The human and professional cost in terms of dignity, family well-being, health, and even continuation in ministry is often calamitously ruinous. Bolton asserts that "conflict is a dangerous opportunity. On an emotional level at least, many of us are more aware of its perils than of its possibilities."[15]

Group Discussion

1. Discuss the freeze response with your group.

2. Have a friendly debate about the consequence of diminished witness and influence of the church in the community due to internal conflict.

3. Why are so many church members so angry? Pinpoint as many possible causes as you can. Suggest possible remedies for the causes you have listed.

Reflection Questions

1. Large, beautiful church buildings punctuate the American landscape. Sadly, however, many of these stately edifices are venues for weekend church fights. From your perspective, what could or should be done to help congregations to recognize the ill-effects of church conflict on the membership and the wider community?

2. As a pastor or ministerial student, take about thirty minutes to think, pray, and write a "note to self" about how your ministry will be different as you think about the matters raised in this chapter. How will you conduct your ministry, going forward? What mistakes have you or others made in the past that you can learn from, going forward?

Notes

1. Robert Bolton, *People Skills: How to Assert Yourself, Listen to Others, and Resolve Conflict* (New York: Simon & Schuster, 1979), 206-207.

2. Timothy Ursiny, *The Coward's Guide to Conflict: Empowering Solutions for Those Who Would Rather Run Than Fight* (Naperville, IL: Sourcebooks, 2003), 27-28.

3. "Walter Bradford Cannon," http://en.wikipedia.org/wiki/Walter_Bradford_Cannon (accessed June 3, 2013).

4. F. Dianne Barth, "Off the Couch: Thoughts about the Therapeutic Process, and the Dynamics of Client-therapist Interactions," http://www.psychologytoday.com/blog/the-couch/ 201210/managing-anxiety-in-the-face-real-danger (accessed June 3, 2013).

5. Runde and Flanagan, *Becoming a Conflict Competent Leader,* 65-80.

6. Norman Shawchuck, *How to Manage Conflict in the Church,* vol. 2 of *Conflict Interventions & Resources,* 5th ed. (Fargo, ND: Spiritual Growth Resources, 2003), 5.

7. Tara Klena Barthel and David V. Edling, *Redeeming Church Conflicts: Turning Crisis into Compassion and Care* (Grand Rapids, MI: Baker Books, 2012), 239.

8. "Statistics in the Ministry," *Pastoral Care Inc.,* http://www.pastoralcareinc. com/statistics (accessed June 3, 2013). (*This reflects 2012 statistics provided by The Fuller Institute, George Barna, and Pastoral Care Inc.*)

9. Ibid.

10. Susek, *Firestorm*, 142.

11. Ibid., 143.

12. Haugk, *Antagonists in the Church*, 32.

13. Alan Nelson and Gene Appel, *How to Change Your Church Without Killing It* (Nashville: Word Publishing, 2000), 231.

14. Ibid.

15. Bolton, People Skills, 207.

CHAPTER 8

Dealing With Belligerent and Abusive Church Members

S ounds like an oxymoron, doesn't it? A belligerent and abusive church member! How on earth (especially in the church) can that possibly be? And yet, most of us who have been in the church for a while have seen it all. We have seen church members fly off the handle in church board or other meetings, cussing, fussing, and being as mean-spirited as they could possibly be toward other members... and even toward their pastor. Some have even thrown physical blows!

Hardly anyone is surprised anymore at the fact that there are church folks who appear to be quite comfortable and even proud of their demonic behaviors and attitudes toward others. The problem is that many have accepted this open manifestation of ungodliness as normative, even necessary. It is not uncommon for some onlookers to nonchalantly offer that, "Well, we all know that's how sister or brother so-and-so is... we just have to love them and pray for one another."

The reality, however, is that verbally abusive and belligerent church members, whether in the pulpit or the pew, are not only a distraction from the power of God's love, but also serve as an unfair and daunting barrier to those who are seeking the Way, the Truth, and the Life that Jesus offers to the lost. Conduct that is clearly inspired by unclean spirits is antithetical to the principles of God's kingdom. While fellow Christians and church leaders should love and pray for those who offend the church and damage the witness of Christ in this way, there is also a biblical obligation for dealing with behavior that undermines the harmony and mission of the church. This is especially true when such conduct negatively impacts the fellowship of the saints and the church becomes a place of tension and pain, rather than a place of fellowship and healing.

I would like to suggest the following principles for dealing with those who damage the social and spiritual fabric of the congregation by behaving like big, bad bullies in the church:

1. Matthew 18:15-20 provides a clearly outlined protocol for dealing with any and all offenses among brethren. This protocol MUST be utilized before anything else is done.

2. Recognize that an abusive and belligerent church member probably has an underlying issue other than the person she or he openly attacks at church (they may target the pastor, some other authority figure, or a fellow member for either no apparent reason, or for petty reasons).

3. Do not sweep this behavior under the rug. It is not likely to go away on its own, especially if it has happened more than once already.

4. It is more likely than not that the member in question also displays these behaviors when not at church. Many verbal abusers and belligerent characters at church are domestic abusers! They emotionally and verbally batter their spouse

and children at home. This needs to be looked into prayerfully and discretely.

5. Give prayerful consideration to the possibility that the abusive member may be dealing with a mental disorder. Not all belligerent behavior is of a spiritual nature only, even though one's spiritual experience may also be a factor. Christians are certainly afflicted by mental illnesses too. **Caution:** This kind of "analysis" of another person is very risky and must be done with the utmost care, being sure to stay within legal and ethical limits as a church leader. Under no circumstance do you want to make statements that could be reasonably construed as legally defamatory, or bordering on the unlawful practice of medicine or psychiatry resulting in legal liability (civil or criminal) on your part about another person, especially and including the very one who may be giving you the hardest time with their own words and behavior. Note: The reader should seek professional legal counsel concerning the above-mentioned reference to "unlawful practice of medicine or psychiatry," which is stated here for awareness and informational purposes only.

6. The abusive person may need to be removed from any church office due to their unrepentance and persistence in wrongdoing. Oftentimes, however, church leaders and other members are afraid to take the necessary action to vacate church offices held by wrong-doers (vote them out), because they fear the verbal and other recrimination that is sure to result.

7. Too many pastors are more worried about who will leave the church when proper and necessary corrective action is taken to reform the church. They should focus instead on the needs of the innocents, and on the right of the church to move on

from its sordid history of damaging conflict, and seek to position the church to become a safe place where people want to be. Let me tell you what the Lord had to tell me... "I called you to protect the sheep, not the wolves who are seeking to devour the sheep!" God had to give me special revelation and wisdom on this matter during one rather challenging period in my ministry, when I was under spiritual attack by Satan via an abusive member. Once that divine priority was settled in my mind, I was emotionally and spiritually prepared to take the necessary steps to remove and constrain the offending member (who refused to repent of his evil behavior, in spite of the obvious consequences of his behavior upon me and the church at large).

8. Educate the church concerning the biblical causes and consequences of abusive behavior among Christians, including in the Christian home. Church members who are more informed and educated concerning the spiritual and other causes of abuse in the church, are more apt at dealing with such occurrences in a timely and decisive (and hopefully redemptive) manner. Don't be afraid to address these issues in the church.

9. Establish and enact a **Code of Conduct** for your church board, clearly outlining what is and what is not acceptable from church officers. In fact, it may be advisable to apply this Code to the entire church, if your fellowship or denomination does not have a church manual which already contains these principles and the steps to be followed if they are violated.

10. Put real teeth into the **Code**, because dentures don't scare church bullies!

11. Heed the biblical injunction to remove an unrepentant person from the church membership. Sometimes as pastors and leaders, we fail to follow divinely given instruction, thinking that our social and psychological sciences and our political correctness are superior to the plain "Thus saith the Lord." In Matthew 18, Jesus, the Head of the church (Colossians 1:18; Ephesians 1:22-23; 5:22-24) said that unrepentant sinners should be removed from the church. The apostle Paul said that those who cause divisions in the church should be noted and shunned! (Romans 16:17-18). Verbal and emotional abuse carries significant consequences for the target of the abuse. This is not a behavior that should be tolerated in the church. It is somewhat ironic that we tend not to discipline people for those evils that actually do the most harm to the most people! Belligerent church abusers are intentional about carrying out their humiliating and wicked design in the most public forum they can find or orchestrate, and they do not care about who gets hurt in the process. Our children and youth who see and hear them in the act of dehumanizing another human being are traumatized by this evil, and many eventually shun the church! This is becoming more noticeable among pastor's kids.

12. Maintain a grace-filled ministry at all times, but be firm when necessary, and consistent in dealing with damaging conduct in the church. Never let it be said that you showed favoritism toward one kind of sin, versus another. A calm, consistent, Christ-like, biblical response to every situation is not only what Christ requires from His leaders, but it is also expected by the members of the church. Many of them will stand with you if you are consistent. Yes, I did say they will stand with you... eventually.

Pastors and other church leaders have a moral responsibility to deliver the church from abusers. It is not permissible to allow any member to openly and persistently harm the church and its mission. Leadership is what most sincere church members are looking for. When the pastor steps up, most Christians will follow.

It should be understood that your church is not a safe place for wrong-doers. If that is what obtains in your church, then it will not be a safe place for the saints and for those who come seeking for an encounter with God.

CHAPTER 9

Something Spectacular Can Arise from the Ashes

One of the primary reasons for me writing this book is the fact that I have seen more than my fair share of congregational conflict, and consequently, have learned much about the subject based on personal experience. Additionally, my doctoral degree is a specialty in Congregational Conflict Resolution Training. My area of specialization was inspired by my pastoral experiences. I have been the target of church conflict, and my leadership and even my character have been called into question. I have endured many amazing experiences, both as a church member, church pastor, and conflict trainer. In the first several years of my ministry, I probably suffered much more from the stress of church conflict than I should have, due to my inability and lack of understanding in recognizing that God was using my experiences to shape me into a more effective church leader, and fashion me for the role I am now widely known for – a conflict minister and conflict ministry trainer.

Good things can come out of bad experiences. The illustrations that I share in this work are all real events that occurred in my pastoral ministry. None is made up. If I did not have these experiences, I would have been at a loss to give my readers applicable living examples of the principles I have shared in this book. At one time, before I was able to value the bad experiences I have had, the burden of conflict with church members and the poor relationships among members that clearly drove people away placed a heavy yoke around my neck and led to serious bouts of disillusionment and discouragement. Mine is the story of many pastors. This is the main reason why so many leave the ministry.

Clearly, the Lord had other plans for my life, to use me in the work of training pastors and churches in the art of congregational conflict resolution. My consulting and training service, CLASS Act Seminars, LLC is the result of this transformed understanding and appreciation on my part for why God allowed me to suffer for a season through congregational conflict. Something good can arise from the ashes after the raging fires of congregational conflict have subsided and you are able to finally realize that God's purpose was not to consume you in the fire, but that the fire was to purify you and make you a fit vessel to be used in wider service for His glory.

While the general results of major conflict are negative, some good can come out of conflicted situations as stated earlier. At first, and in the heat of emotional battle, positive lessons or outcomes may not appear possible, but Strauch offers that:

> It is helpful to keep in mind that there is nothing wrong
> with Christians disagreeing with one another or pas-
> sionately defending our beliefs. This is how we learn,
> how we sharpen and correct our thinking, and how
> we help others improve. The Holy Spirit often uses
> the emotional upheaval that accompanies disagree-
> ments and conflict to get our attention and drive us
> to make necessary changes in our families, churches,
> and personal lives. Conflict can help us to discover

our character weaknesses, correct mistaken theological ideas, sharpen our beliefs, refine our plans, grow in wisdom and life experience, learn to trust God during difficult times, and deepen our prayer lives.[1]

Runde and Flanagan contend that,

The most effective leaders are extraordinarily competent at handling conflict . . . they respond to conflict constructively. In doing so, they not only keep potentially damaging situations under control, they discover options, solutions, and possibilities previously unseen or unknown. They learn to embrace conflict not as an organizational enemy but as an opportunity for growth and a source of creative energy.[2]

Nelson and Appel agree with the plausibility of positive outcomes from conflict, urging that "how you handle anger and disagreements as a church family is a huge lesson on life and spiritual growth."[3] These points made by these various writers are all good principles to keep in mind and to practice. So often, conflict in the church only reaps the negative results. With a more enlightened approach to conflict ministry, church leaders and members should be able to seize upon the potential for good that conflict presents.

For Conference and Other Denominational Leaders

1. Based on the principles shared in this chapter, how do you think pastors can benefit from more exposure to conflict ministry before graduation from ministerial training programs?

2. What opportunities exist for the conference, the pastor, and the church in situations where there is major conflict in churches?

Reflection Questions

1. Local Elders – Describe a time when there was major conflict in your local congregation. Talk about how the matter was handled by the pastor, board of elders, and the conference. How was it concluded?

Notes

1. Alexander Strauch, *If You Bite and Devour One Another: Biblical Principles for Handling Conflict* (Littleton, CO: Lewis and Roth Publishers, 2011), 3.

2. Runde and Flanagan, *Becoming a Conflict Competent Leader*, 115.

3. Nelson and Appel, *How to Change Your Church*, 239.

PART THREE

TRANSITIONING A CONFLICTED CONGREGATION

CHAPTER 10

From Holy Hell to Hallelujah Again

I started this book by sharing my personal testimony about my initiation into pastoral ministry. For the first three years in my first assignment, I called my conference president each year, pleading with him to "get me out of here!" I would call him back the very next day to tell him that "the Lord didn't tell me to tell you that… that was me talking out of my frustration. I don't want to leave. I need to be here, because this church needs to change!" Within two years of being in the ministry, I became very ill, but no physiological cause could be found after several examinations, including me being tested for cancer. My body was hurting all over without explanation. Finally, one specialist asked me the question, "What do you do for a living?" When I replied that "I am a pastor," the doctor threw both hands into the air, shook his head, and stoutly declared, "That's your problem! I have seen this before. Your problem is stress!"

To be perfectly honest, while I felt a great sense of relief at knowing that there was a reasonable and curable cause for the myriad of health issues I had been struggling with for several months, I was also embarrassed that "I had allowed" the stresses of my ministry, my calling, to get to me so badly that I almost lost my life. That experience shook me up rather badly. My ministry in that certain church had become somewhat of a holy hell.

It was in the midst of dealing with my embarrassment and depression at being nearly killed by my job, a job that was portrayed as leading people who love God… that I began to seriously ponder the inadequacy of my ministerial training. I had completed my four-year Bachelor's Degree in Pastoral Theology, followed by my two-year Master of Divinity Degree with emphasis on Church Growth and Evangelism. Then I was hired and assigned without any kind of orientation to the particular church. No one from the conference briefed me on conditions that I would encounter in the church. It did not take long for me to discover that the conference leaders knew just about everything that was happening there, yet not a word was said to me. Two years of Greek and one year of Hebrew studies, several courses in Church History, and many other courses that I now barely remember doing were required of me in my academic training, but not even ten minutes of training in conflict resolution was introduced to me. Yet, this was the most essential tool that I would actually need on a weekly basis throughout my ministry.

Ministry became my emotional hell, as the consuming flames of conflict overwhelmed me almost from day one. I soon began to "threaten" God that I would never again speak in His name, feeling that He had tricked me into the ministry. It was a nightmare. I would pray the forty miles to church (this was one of two congregations under my care) and cry thirty-nine miles back toward my house. That's because there was a gas station a mile from home where I would stop to wipe my tears and get myself together so that my wife (who refused to attend that church for a while) would not have to see the terrible shape that her husband was coming back from church in.

After my physically and emotionally painful encounter with compromised health had passed, my desperation and determination combined to inspire me to launch out on a very urgent quest to learn and understand how to survive the fires of congregational conflict. I had been sent to a war zone without a proper briefing or adequate training, and some of the wrong-doers in the church soon tried to tag me as the cause of the church's turmoil (even though the church had a wide renown as a problem church, as I would shortly discover). I was now very determined to survive and thrive where I had been sent. I was going to beat the odds. I would not be driven away!

This book is a brief (don't laugh out too loudly) summary of years of pastoral experience and doctoral research. Later in this chapter, I will share some specific steps that may be of help to pastors, local church elders, church boards, and board of trustees; also conference leaders who are tasked with selecting pastors and overseeing congregations, and college professors who are tasked with training young people to become pastors. It is my prayer that the strategies shared here will be a blessing to many churches, and will help pastors all over the world to learn how to survive church conflict.

Three-and-a-half years after I was assigned to that church, I could happily report that the transition of the congregation was accomplished. A piece of work had miraculously become a class act! A holy hell had become hallelujah again! It was realized mainly through much trial and error, and with many tears and nights of prayer. There were many sleepless nights because of stress and depression, as I wrestled with the question of how to turn around a church from vicious conflict to Christian love. Finally, God gave the breakthrough! It was hard work, and it took a personal toll on me emotionally and physically (not to mention financially due to the medical expenses that I incurred). Nevertheless, that congregation eventually became one of the best overall pastorates I have had. We became a missional and growing church. When I was transferred, I had achieved the distinction of being the longest serving pastor in their more than seventy year history, serving for six years and nine months! They have invited me back several times since we left.

Even though many writers promote the idea of conflict resolution, I should caution that all conflict will not be resolved. In recognition of this reality, McSwain and Treadwell talk of "concluding conflict."[1] Some conflicts will be concluded by one of the conflicted parties leaving the church, or both agreeing to end open hostilities, even though agreement on the issue may never be reached and hard feelings may even continue to be privately harbored. Poirier challenges that "Christian conflict theory must be theologically rooted and ecclesiastically integrated."[2] This is critical if conflict is to be correctly and biblically concluded.

I hold the view that conflict is prolonged and becomes damaging to the church due to the general lack of willingness on the part of most Christians to obey the biblical protocol for resolving conflict. I will give more specific and detailed insights on this in the next section of this book.

Let us now turn our attention to strategies for transitioning a conflicted congregation. I should point out that this is my model that works for me. Some of these steps may be uncomfortable for some readers. Not only is this strategy being shared only as a suggested approach, it is also not claimed to be an exhaustive list of steps. Perhaps you the reader have tried and proven another method of accomplishing what I have been able to successfully achieve using these steps. It should be noted also that every church may not need every step in this strategy. Congregational conditions and needs vary; therefore the reader should contextualize this recommendation before using it. Suffice it to say also, that the personality and temperament of the pastor will also factor into determining what approach is used, and how it will be implemented. As a conflict trainer, I recognize and am sensitive to the role that personality plays in the conflict process. The following is what has worked for me:

The Role of Church Leadership in the Transition Process

<u>The Pastor</u>

An adequately prepared pastor is a great asset to any church, but especially one that is dealing with damaging conflict and needs to transition from holy hell to hallelujah again. It is my view that the overwhelming majority of conflicts in the typical congregation actually preceded the pastor's arrival, especially those churches that rotate pastors through the denominational transfer system (such as the Seventh-day Adventist Church, the Methodist Church, and the Presbyterian Church). This would also apply to congregational churches that experience average to higher than average pastoral turnover. While it is true that pre-existing conflict often escalates under the leadership of a pastor who has not been trained in conflict ministry (which is most pastors), we need to be sure to not unfairly saddle the pastor with unjustifiable blame for these conflicts.

The pastor is the assigned leader of the church. Regardless of the conditions he or she inherits, once installed as the pastor, the weight of responsibility now shifts to him or her as the leader. It is now his or her burden to shoulder. However, I want to clearly establish at this juncture that no one person can pastor (nurture, minister, take care of) a church. That is impossible. I also want to establish that the first responsibility of the pastor is to protect the church. Some may disagree with this view, arguing that feeding the church comes first. However, it is my strategy to protect by feeding, and to strengthen the people by informing and inspiring them so that they will not be ignorant to the tactics of the destroyer. I will say more on this in the next step on establishing a biblical foundation for change.

In any meaningful organization or entity, leadership is critical to success. It is very unlikely that a church will do well without an effective leader. By the same token, an effective leader is one who empowers and equips his fellow leaders for team ministry in the local church. The pastor must have a vision of what even a terribly conflicted church can become. He has to be able to articulate that vision and capture the imagination of the church. He must be able to inspire hope in a change from a state of holy hell to hallelujah again.

Pastors who are properly trained and denominationally empowered can do a more excellent work in conflict ministry. My strategy has been to immediately organize the elders into what I call the pastoral staff, by vote of the church. The term "pastoral staff" typically applies where there are two or more clergy on staff at the church, however, in my context as a Seventh-day Adventist, most pastors are not only the only clergy overseeing the congregation, but most pastors are assigned to more than one church. We refer to this arrangement as a "district," hence my need to empower the elders and insure that both they and the membership as a whole understand that while they are not assistant pastors, they are in fact pastoral assistants.

I am also aware that in many faith communions, they enjoy the benefit of a multi-pastor staff, in addition to a team of elders as their norm. A minority of Seventh-day Adventist churches also enjoy this benefit due to the size of their membership. In any event, I would advise that the elders of the church be viewed and even drafted into the official pastoral staff, as there is much good to be gained from the entire leadership team working in even closer cooperation for the good of the church.

My motivation is the biblical teaching on the priesthood of all believers (1 Peter 2:1-10). It was never God's intention that any one man or woman, or only a few folks should assume the heavy burdens of all the people. Exodus 18 is very instructive in this regard. This is why I am intentional in elevating the role of the elder, sending a clear message to the congregation that I cannot do the work of pastoring all of them all by myself. I am very open with my views in this regard. Pastors are human beings too, with strengths that are sometimes celebrated, but we also have weaknesses, limitations and flaws. I organize the elders into a consultative team, and hold bi-weekly pastoral staff meetings. These meetings are very important and a blessing to my leadership strategy and effectiveness.

In the pastoral staff meetings, I also train the elders in the art of conflict ministry so that they can assist me in adjudicating the cases of conflict between members. This way, most disputes in the church do not end up on my desk. I carefully heed Jethro's counsel to Moses in Exodus 18. In the staff meetings, we also counsel and consult together about members who are of concern perhaps due to absenteeism, those who are sick and shut in, those who are disgruntled, and those who are not doing as well as expected in leading ministries. These meetings are very productive, in that I am able to see and understand more about each situation that we address simply because the elders have been a part of the congregation much longer than I have, and they know the nuances of most situations and can provide me with sound advice on how to approach each matter.

As a leader, I have matured significantly throughout my years of ministry. I attribute this fact to three primary reasons; (1) my passion for the gospel ministry which highly motivates me to continually study the ministry through avid research, (2) my advanced educational preparation arising from my doctoral pursuits, and (3) the many experiences that my pastoral journey have afforded me – I have been very intentional about learning from all my experiences.

The leader's total commitment to Jesus, his vision, his stamina for hard work, wisdom, courage, patience, tack, skill, firmness, and grace-filled manner of dealing with people (even those who err) will make a great difference in the church. As the pastor, I must resolve in my heart that this work is not about me. It is entirely about what God wants to do for His people. He works through me to bless others. It is an undeserved honor and a great privilege to be chosen by God to pastor His people. I must, as their pastor, take care of them. I must teach the elders to help me take care of them. I must trust, empower, mobilize and authorize the elders to be my equal ministry partners in caring for the church, the people of God.

Whenever I am installed in a new church, the first order of business for me is to see about the state of the local leadership. I am very clear about this one thing - churches rise or fall on leadership. Elders are indispensable to my work as a pastor.

The Elders

Through my CLASS Act Seminars ministry, I get many calls to conduct elders' training in churches around the country and outside of the USA also. This group of leaders in the local church is very important to the success of the congregation. Unfortunately, I estimate that perhaps more than ninety percent of all damaging church conflicts originate in or escalate among the leadership of the church and then filter down to the congregation. My burden, and a large part of my work as a leadership and conflict trainer, is helping pastors and elders to accept and utilize the fact that we are a team.

I use the illustration of a football team in my workshops to demonstrate the importance of the leadership structure of the church and what it is for. I regard the pastor as the quarterback of the team. He is the captain. He calls the plays on the field. In the Seventh-day Adventist Church we use the conference system of denominational governance. In our case, the conference would be the coaching staff. Though they are a vital part of the operation of the team, they are not in the trenches with the pastor doing frontline ministry in the local church. The elders are the offensive line, whose task it is to protect the quarterback. The quarterback has the football (the Word of God and the weighty responsibility as the one who watches out for the souls of the members).

Imagine what would happen in a football game if the offensive linesmen suddenly turn around and start rushing their own quarterback! The spectators would think that they are all mad. In fact, the coaching staff would go ballistic! Imagine how the owners would react to what they're witnessing on the field! By the way, did I mention that the owners are in the skybox watching the game? That's God the Father, the Son, and the Holy Spirit, to Whom the church belongs, up in heaven watching over the church. The Owners are watching the team self-destruct in the middle of the game! This would be contrary to the Owners' plan! Remember, Jesus guaranteed that "the gates of hell shall not prevail against" the church!

Funny as it may sound, this is exactly what is happening in many churches. There is conflict among the pastors and elders or the other local leaders of the church. In many cases, there is rancor between the pastor and the board of trustees. It is our collective responsibility to protect the football, and to see to it that the pastor can get it down-field to the receivers (church members) to score touchdowns for the kingdom of God. We have to fix the leadership of the church. Nothing is happening until we do. This may mean that some elders will have to be removed from the team. Sometimes it may mean that we need a new quarterback. It may mean that all would have to be retrained. Good leadership is essential for transitioning a church.

One crucial aspect of congregational leadership is clarifying and defining leadership roles. Sometimes, the origin of conflict is not personal, but structural. If leadership team members are unclear of their roles, it is very likely that there will be conflict as folks start operating in other people's lanes. The pastor, as the team leader, is responsible for seeing that every team member has a specific ministry assignment. This needs to be in writing and agreed to by the pastor and the team members. In my ministry, I assign the elders to specific functions. This assignment is based upon two factors, (1) the elder's skill set, and (2) what we are seeking to accomplish that year. I should point out that the assignments are not permanent, but may vary from year to year, based on need.

The head elder is always my pastoral assistant for administration. He or she is responsible, among other things, for seeing to the implementation of all voted actions of the church board. Of course, I do not totally abandon or recuse myself from participating in this function, but it is mainly the head elder's responsibility to follow up with everyone who is asked to enact a decision, and see that it is done within the specified time. Another function that my head elder serves is to insure that the "lead elder" (one is assigned for each week's worship service) has done his or her duty to call and confirm every participant on the worship program for that week. I require that worship program participants be called (though they were given the schedule for the quarter) no later than Monday each week to be reminded and to confirm their attendance before the church bulletin is printed on Wednesday.

I cannot overstate the importance of assigning staff members to roles that match their spiritual gifts. Placing someone in a position that they are not suited for is unfair to them and counter-productive for the church. The pastor's ministry will surely suffer for it too.

Crafting well thought-out and widely publicized protocols for carrying out both administrative and ministry functions is another crucial aspect of congregational leadership. It is one thing to say what should be done, but quite another to insure that people know how it should be done or who is responsible for doing it. This is where many leaders fail, and confusion is the inevitable result. Lack of thoughtfully crafted and well publicized protocols is known to cause untold frustration in the body. Leadership team members should not only be assigned to tasks, but should be informed about how and perhaps when those tasks should be done. I hold my elders accountable for assignments; therefore it is only fair to them that they know what I expect from them. It is better to write it down to insure compliance.

The leadership and organizational structure of the church determines, to a certain extent, the level of efficiency and effectiveness of the leadership team and officers of the church. It therefore needs to be periodically reviewed and refined to insure that it is the best system to deliver services to the members and to those who have an interest in becoming members.

Establish a Biblical Foundation for Change

People are naturally skeptical of change. That's not some people, but all people. Every single one of us shrinks from some kinds of change at least some of the times. Interestingly, change is mostly palatable to those who initiate it. However, the initiators or "change agents" also naturally chafe at changes that are initiated by others. Pastors, by the very nature of the ministry, must initiate changes from time to time that may to some extent cause church members to chafe a bit. This reaction is normal, natural, and mostly healthy. It is human nature. This reality should not cause the pastor to usher in a ministry characterized by a "no change" policy, but it should serve as a reminder that change needs to be "properly" managed.

The word "properly" is somewhat subjective, I am sure. However, my usage of it is to suggest that change should not be done merely for the sake of change, and without regard for the effect that it will have on the church. Change should be carefully studied, planned, and wisely implemented. Granted, regardless of how careful the pastor is, no matter how tactful his approach to leading change, a certain percentage of members will complain, and some will even seek to undermine the change effort. My purpose here is mainly to show the importance of having and demonstrating a legitimate need to change. Most people will adapt to change if they can see the rationale and the need. When the benefits of the proposed change outweigh the cost (emotional, financial, loss of convenience, discomfort with losing a cherished tradition) of the change, you can move forward with the change process successfully. When there is conflict in the church, change for the better is always welcome! It is the pastor's role, with the assistance of the elders, to make the case for necessary change.

The most notable spiritual transformation experiences have always begun with a discovered or re-discovered biblical mandate. Two great examples of this can be found in the 2 Kings 22 and Nehemiah 8. In the first instance, young King Josiah enacted much needed reforms after Hilkiah the High Priest "found the Book of the Law in the house of the Lord." Many years later, when the broken down condition of Jerusalem had been repaired by Nehemiah, Ezra the priest brought the Book of the Law of Moses from the house of God to be read in the hearing of all the people. As a result of both of these incidents, there was a great spiritual awakening among the people of God. Both incidents signaled a transition from apostasy to repentance. Both marked a turning point in the corporate spiritual journey of the people of God.

The pastor's whims, good intentions, or desire to copy some other church, are not good enough reasons to justify generating the resistance and conflict that will probably result from efforts to implement change. The Bible teaches the need for change that will transform hearts and transition churches from being hotbeds of conflict to class act congregations. What would a biblical foundation for the spiritual and relational transition of a church look like?

Central to any cause or movement, is the important question, "Why?" Why does the church exist? Why are conflicted churches a bad idea? Why is a change needed? Why must there be a transition from a state of holy hell? Let's answer these questions from the Bible's perspective. As stated before, the type of change that is involved in transitioning a conflicted church should not be initiated based upon someone's whim, but should be in response to a divine mandate in order to succeed. So what has the Lord said to the church through the Bible? What is the foundation of this necessary change?

The church is not a man-made entity. We have already established that God created the church and appointed Jesus Christ to be the Head of the church. Jesus declared that He built the church or the kingdom of grace upon Himself, the Rock. The foundation of the church is Jesus Christ. The church exists for the purpose of representing Jesus to the world, to call people out of darkness into the marvelous light of relationship with God. In order to succeed in fulfilling our purpose, Jesus said that the people we represent Him to must be convinced that we are in fact, His representatives. Upon what evidence then, will they rely, in order to believe our testimony about the power of God to transform their lives? According to Jesus, they will believe us when they see how we demonstrate love to one another as members of the body of Christ (John 13:34, 35).

Conflicted churches are bad press for the kingdom of grace. The sad reality of Youtube videos of pastors and church members slapping each other's face on the side of the road with the church steeple serving as the video background, church members dragging each other into court, and newspapers and television stories making fun of the church because of comedic drama in the church is despicable. I don't blame the press. They are doing their job by reporting the news. It is the church's fault why we are the news and in the news for the wrong reasons. Our purpose, our calling is to share the gospel, the good news about the fact that "God so loved the world that He gave His only begotten Son, that whosoever believes in Him should not perish, but have everlasting life." The news further states that "God did not send His Son into the world to condemn the world, but that the world through Him might be saved!" That's our purpose! Unfortunately, Christ is being more misrepresented than represented by many churches.

Bringing this sense of purpose before the people of God, by urging them to prayerfully ponder our biblical mandate to be harbingers of good news, is sure to gradually generate a corporate sense of repentance. We can initiate change by demonstrating very graphically where we are as a church in comparison to where God has called us to be… and all we need to do is read the Bible. We can show the people Paul's admonition in Ephesians 4 (the entire chapter). Most church members are more interested in reading chapter 5 so as to be able to get into heated, unproductive arguments about the role of women in the home and the church, and completely skip over chapter 4 that deals with relationships and unity. This is how deceptive the Devil is!

Ephesians 4 can help in a powerful way to lay out the call of God for a unified church. 1 Corinthians 13, the great chapter on love, is indispensable to the conversation at hand. Space does not permit me to delve into the multitudinous amount of counsel enshrined in the Scriptures that the astute pastor and supporting cast of elders can use for sermons and Bible studies to bring awareness to the people of God for why the church must change from being a holy hell to hallelujah again!

Review and Refine the Church Administrative Structure

Earlier in this book, I stated that the origin of church conflict is not always personal, but sometimes structural. In some instances, the internal administrative systems of the church may hinder instead of enable people in their efforts to conduct the business and ministries of the church. Leaders need to ask and honestly answer the following questions: How are decisions made? Who is responsible for making this decision or that decision? Is there a clearly defined chain of command? How many meetings are required before relatively small amounts of money can be spent? Does the pastor have to sign off on every decision? Are there others, apart from the pastor, who share in the day-to-day administration of the church's business? Is there a provision for expending funds without board approval in cases of emergency? Is there a written job description for all members of the pastoral staff, the church treasurer, the church secretary? What procedures are to be followed to plan special programs, invite speakers, spend ministry funds from departments, and use the various church facilities? What procedures are to be followed if people need to request financial assistance? Who should be contacted if there is a medical emergency among the church family? In event of a death, what should be done, and who is supposed to do it? Do people have to contact the pastor to request help or permission for opening the church for a program? The defining questions for this review of the church's administrative structure and protocols or procedures are what, why, who, when, and how?

I have seen cases where conflict ensued because there was not enough information in general circulation about the what, why, who, when, and how. These are important details to pay attention to. Much frustration and confusion can be avoided or eliminated if a careful review of roles and protocols is done periodically. I would suggest that these questions be discussed in the pastoral staff meeting, and then specific recommendations for improvement be brought to the church board for discussion and action. Even if we believe that everything is going well, this audit of our systems is essential. We don't normally realize how much better we can be until we start asking questions about the way we've always done it.

The Church Election, a Key Component of Church Transition

This is one of my favorite but most easily botched steps in the church transitioning process. Let me get right to it. Church office does not belong to anyone! The pastor serves as a privilege afforded and extended to him or her. Being a pastor is not a right. I am not entitled to serve in this office, nor am I worthy of the privilege. It is an honor for me to serve, and it brings a sense of humility with it. This is God's Church. It baffles me that people are possessive about church office. Holding church office is a call to servant leadership. Now, I must point out that servant leadership is not code for treating those who serve badly. In fact, the Bible teaches that those who serve well should be honored (the context is how to treat elders, with whom pastors are linked, according to Peter, but by extension, every member who serves well deserves to be highly regarded).

In too many cases, church conflict originates among those who hold office in the church. An exaggerated sense of self-importance usually fuels egos that result in conflict. Holding church office can be harmful to one's soul! If not properly managed, our emotional attachment to what we do for God can become the very thing that sours our attitudes and hence undermines our effectiveness.

Most people do not like or respond well to church officers who are known for a sour attitude. Complaining, murmuring, half-stepping church officers just don't cut it. In my ministry, I have no choice but to insist on excellence. I let it be known that I'm not authorized to accept anything less. We work for God. I will say more about this later. Pastors work very hard to build up the ministry where they serve. They have a lot riding on the condition of the church under their stewardship. Pastors are judged based upon church members' and denominational leaders' perception of their stewardship over the church. It is therefore unfair that other people, who are not held to the same level of scrutiny and accountability, and who normally have no consequences to face when the ministry fails to realize expectations, are allowed to harm the pastor's ministry by having a mediocre approach to their own ministry responsibilities.

Every church officer's performance or lack thereof affects the people's perception of the pastor's leadership effectiveness and his overall stewardship as the church's leader. This is a matter that I take very seriously, and therefore conduct periodic evaluations of all ministries and ministry leaders. I have a strict operating principle that I abide by – "Any attitude or performance that can get you fired from your secular job, may be cause to remove you from the office you hold in this church. If it is not accepted at your job, it will not be accepted here." This is about mutual accountability. Too many church members have been led to believe that they can criticize, judge, abuse, fight and undermine the pastor, when they themselves contribute very little to the advancement of the church. They tear down rather than build up the body, and then blame the pastor for the failing efforts of the church. Members who hold church office are especially prone to this kind of destructive behavior, even while they fail to faithfully carry out the roles they were elected to fulfill. I will say more on this later.

The church election provides an opportunity to scrutinize all ministry leaders and functions, and to make a determination about where we want to go and who is best suited to help us get there. In the Seventh-day Adventist Church, local churches in a given geographical region are organized into administrative/oversight units or organizations called a Conference. These conferences have a team of Executive Officers consisting of a President, an Executive Secretary (or Vice President for Administration), a Treasurer (or Vice President of Finance), and maybe a General Vice President (varies from conference to conference). There is a Ministerial Director (alternately called a Vice President of Pastoral Ministries), and several departmental directors of specialized ministries such as Youth Ministries, Personal Ministry and Sabbath School, Stewardship and Trust Services, Women and Children, Public Affairs and Religious Liberty, Communication, etc.

Local conferences within a wider geographical region are grouped together into a Union Conference, such as my home territory in the Southern Union Conference of Seventh-day Adventists (Southeastern United States). There are currently one hundred and fifty Union Conferences in the worldwide Seventh-day Adventist Church. All of our Unions around the world make up what we refer to as the General Conference of Seventh-day Adventists, the administrative body that coordinates our global ministry efforts. The General Conference functions through its thirteen world Divisions, such as the North American Division of the Seventh-day Adventist Church, which has administrative jurisdiction over the work in Bermuda, Canada, Guam-Micronesia, and the United States of America.

Each level of the denomination has regular Constituency Sessions at which Officers and Departmental Directors are elected by delegates. They serve in their respective capacities for a term of five years at the Union Conference (Union) and General Conference (GC) levels, whereas local conferences have terms of office that vary from three to five years, in accordance with their individual constitutions. Officers for the Divisions of the GC are also elected during the GC Session every five years. Division Presidents are Vice Presidents of the GC.

My purpose for sharing this information (apart from the fact that I am proud of the global gospel, education, healthcare and humanitarian ministry of our church) is to inform you, the reader, that at every level of the World Church from the local Conference to the GC, when the nominating committee recommends a person for the office of President, and the constituency by vote elects the individual as President, he is invited and given the courtesy of sitting with the nominating committee to "advise" and "counsel" with them concerning the makeup of the rest of the slate of officers and departmental directors that shall come before the delegates in the session. The President is perhaps most intentional about who is selected to be the Executive Secretary, the officer who is informally understood to be "next to the presidency" even though it is not so written in the "Law of the Medes and the Persians" of Adventist polity.

It only makes sense that the President is not forced to work with whoever the delegates chose to elect to serve with him. He should rightly be given the courtesy of having input in the selection of his cabinet. After all, he is the one (after the delegates disperse back to their own lives and churches) who will have to work with this team for the next five years. The other reason I shared this information is to let you know that the only level of the organization where this protocol (even though there is no policy against doing so) is not likewise followed, is during local church elections!

Remember, congregational conflict occurs only at the local

church level… at the congregation! In our system (by policy), the pastor is the chairperson of the church nominating committee. Several years ago, I changed my method of conducting the church election. The first step in the process is where I call the business meeting (voted at the 2015 GC Session to be called the constituency meeting of the church) for the purpose of electing the organizing committee. This committee recommends the nominating committee to be approved by vote of the church in constituency meeting.

At the beginning of the church constituency meeting, I ask the Clerk to read the sections of the Church Manual regarding the qualifications for holding church office. I then advise the members that "since we are not here to embarrass anyone in these proceedings, please do not nominate any person to serve on the organizing (large) committee (they select the nominating committee) who we all know does not meet these qualifications. Individuals who are known to be <u>in open violation</u> of these principles do not qualify to serve. If you nominate such a person, I am not authorized to accept the nomination, and will have no choice but to say to you that 'The Chair (I use the third person, because it's not personal) cannot accept that nomination, do you have another name?'"

What is my justification for formulating this approach? It is found in the following statement in the "Elections" chapter of our Church Manual, under the sub-title "Who Should Be Members of the Nominating Committee." It states, "Only members in <u>regular standing</u> should be chosen to serve on the nominating committee. They should be <u>persons of good judgment</u> who have the welfare and <u>prosperity of the church at heart</u>." (emphasis supplied). Let us unpack this statement and seek to understand how I use this policy to effect necessary change in the transitioning process.

The term "regular standing" is used several times in the Church

Manual, but is unfortunately, not defined. This is a cause of concern for me, since it appears to suggest that as long as a member is not currently under some form of church discipline, he is considered to be in "regular standing." This is problematic, seeing that in most churches, the wrong-doers who are causing discord and undermining the peace in the church are usually not disciplined! In fact, in my experience, the church has been rather quick to remove the names of "other types of sinners" from the membership roll, but is unwilling to touch those who have a long history of damaging the church through conflict.

Some of these individuals have been guilty of verbally abusing pastors and other leaders and members. Many of them have slandered their leaders, and have been allowed to remain in church office without any kind of consequences or without demonstrating any remorse or repentance. This is because the members have been too afraid to hold them accountable. There is no way that we can honestly conclude that these individuals are in regular standing! Therefore, I use this Church Manual statement to instruct and empower the membership to exclude any person from the election process who demonstrates a destructive spirit of discord.

The good news is that no one has ever fought me for using this approach. As a result of this approach, I have not ended up with any person of questionable regard for the welfare and prosperity of the church on the organizing or nominating committee. Think about it… an individual who has high regard for the welfare and prosperity of the church will not intentionally do anything to cast the church in a negative light or seek to destroy the pastor or his ministry. So yes, there are effective ways to manage the election process and use the process to eradicate some of the problems that have dogged the church for years. My members have been grateful that finally, a strong pastor has come, one who is willing to take a stand and take the church back from the bullies who have held the people of God hostage for years.

My method is simple. If the pastor and the congregation allow just anyone to get on the organizing committee, they will elect themselves to the nominating committee, and ultimately to church offices. Holding office places them on the church board. They will therefore have a platform for continuing to exert their destructive influence in the church. My strategy is to provide strong leadership and empower the members to take responsibility for, and participate in transitioning the church from holy hell to hallelujah again!

With regard to choosing elders for the church, I recommend the individuals for the office of elder to the nominating committee. I then open it up for any other names that the committee may want to consider for that position. It is rare that any other name is added to the slate of elders, as the committee usually allows me the benefit of serving with men and women who have demonstrated the spiritual maturity and godly commitment that is necessary for effective ministry. The elders of the church are assistants to the pastor. It is only logical that the pastor has a say in who is chosen for this important position, seeing that he must rely heavily on them for support as burden bearers and problem solvers. In doing this, I have simply implemented the same approach in local church elections as is done in elections at every other level of the church.

As a result of my method for doing church elections, we do not have acrimonious church board meetings! It simply does not happen ever since I changed my approach. My board members know that I have the utmost respect for those who serve with me, but they also know that I expect their respect in return. There is no substitute for mutual respect for each other and the utmost respect for God and for the Church and its mission that He has entrusted to our care.

Develop a Mission Statement

A church mission statement is absolutely necessary. Think about it this way – you probably won't accomplish your mission if you don't know what it is! This is not optional for a church that is serious about realizing its purpose. A few notes on the mission statement: (1) it should not be longer than John 3:16, so that the church's children can recite it; (2) it should be Christ-centered and community focused; (3) it should be printed in your weekly church bulletin; (4) it should form the basis of the church's strategic plan; (5) it should inform everything the church does; (6) it should be recited periodically during the worship service and scroll on the screen every week; and (7) it should be revisited and refined as needed at least every three to five years to insure relevance.

The mission statement helps in a powerful way to point the church in a more desirable direction. A clear sense of purpose is a great way to motivate the members. When they have a meaningful focus to rally around, they will be less inclined to get caught up in the other stuff. People get excited about the prospect of going somewhere that they clearly see and understand. Too many churches are just a routine that people do because it's what they're expected to do. There is no sense of purpose, no vision of something greater than sinful self-absorption. Selfishness is at the very heart of church conflicts. Give the people something to look forward to doing for the kingdom of God. Create a mission statement.

The Importance of a Strategic Plan

Any church that creates a strong mission statement will very soon afterward realize that they need a road map, some kind of written guide containing measurable goals, events, benchmarks, and a method for evaluating their outcomes if they are ever going to accomplish their mission. This is called a strategic plan. I recommend it! In fact, I fail to see how any church can exist without a strategic plan. A strategic plan promotes unity and mission focus.

No matter how wonderful sounding the mission statement, if there is no specific plan in place to accomplish the stated mission, it is nothing but words on a piece of paper. The church cannot afford to simply exist. We are called by God to "go into all the world and make disciples..." We are to "show forth the praises of Him who called us out of darkness into his marvelous light." That sounds like action to me. A strategic plan builds on the mission statement by providing the specific steps that will lead the church to the realization of its purpose. The plan should always be contextual. This means that the plan for a pastoral colleagues' church in the next city or state will not do. You and your church need to engage in the hard work of prayerfully (and with fasting) seeking God to find out His will for your particular ministry in your local context. I read somewhere that "The LORD is near to all them that call on him..."

The Church Board Code of Conduct

For reasons that still defy my ability to understand, people like to fight in church board meetings! I simply don't get it. The meeting opens with a prayer, and then... there's nothing but holy hell! Anger, ugly attitudes, disrespect, fussing, and sometimes even fist fights characterize the board room in many churches. Many board members refuse to attend because it is too depressing to witness the vitriol that passes for passion for the church.

Many church constituency meetings (referred to as conferences in some faith communions) also rapidly disintegrate as soon as the session opens. Why do people behave this way? Why do people who claim to have the love of Jesus in their hearts put on such a demoralizing display of devilment? And in the church house at that!

The answer is rather complex. Some factors to consider include, but are not limited to: (1) personality disorders or mental illness; (2) spiritual and emotional immaturity; (3) lack of understanding of the purpose of a board meeting; (4) confusion about who the enemy is; (5) the church's error in choosing officers based on their spiritual gifts regardless of whether the individual also possesses the fruit of the Spirit; (6) lack of accountability and consequences for unruly, destructive behavior; (7) lack of training in conflict resolution; (8) inadequate church board orientation and training; (9) demon possession and (10) the passive response of pastors who are afraid to assert the authority that comes with the biblical Office of the Pastor.

After each election is completed and the new church board is seated, I present and ask the board to vote the Church Board Code of Conduct. This is a document that fills in the blanks left by the Church Manual and speaks specifically to this church's needs. Among other things, the Code holds all board members, including me as the pastor, to a standard of care and conduct that promotes civility, mutual respect, and care for the church. I mentioned earlier that I am not authorized by God to tolerate any conduct that diminishes any member and undermines the mission of the church. Remember, the first responsibility of the pastor is to protect the church! That sometimes means that pastors have to protect the church from members who just don't get it.

In fairness to my pastoral colleagues, I am aware that most have probably never heard it said this way before. Ministerial training focuses primarily of the preaching of the gospel. That is why we are required to do so much Greek, Hebrew, homiletics, hermeneutics, public speaking, and all those other wonderful courses that develop the more "up front" competencies. That is all well and good, but I challenge that approach in contemporary pastoral training with this thought: What the church needs in the 21st Century is not more great preachers, but pastors who know how to lead a church. Moses,

Nehemiah, and Joshua were not preachers. They were great leaders. I can imagine the ferocious backlash to this statement just about now, but before you get mad, consider carefully what I just said.

I am not at all advocating that we do not need men and women who know how to skillfully divide the Word of God and make it plain to the people in a manner that makes them cry, "What must we do to be saved?" What I am suggesting is that it takes skillful leadership to transition and take a church forward. People cannot hear the gospel because of the confusion in our conflicted churches. Jesus said the people will be convinced that we are His representatives if we demonstrate to them that we love one another. Pastors have to become better leaders of change and also learn how to conduct conflict ministry in the 21st Century Church.

The two groups of members that the pastor works more closely with are the elders and the church board (board of trustees in some places). In these two settings, the astute, determined pastor has the opportunity to effect and manage transitional principles that will help the church to move from holy hell to hallelujah again. I urge pastors to seize and utilize this opportunity quickly, firmly, and lovingly. Please see Exhibit A in the Appendix for an example of the Church Board Code of Conduct that you may freely adapt and use.

Teach and Affirm the Church's Official Doctrinal Beliefs

Earlier in this book, I showed that one category of cause for congregational conflict is theological disputes. This is actually more common that it is rare. I would recommend to pastors that even if theological or doctrinal conflicts are not your current concern, still plan to do a full teaching series at least every other year for the sake of insuring that the members know and understand what the church officially believes.

Church members in the 21st Century are largely uninformed or ill-informed about the Bible. Chances are there are significant numbers in your local congregation who are not well versed in the official doctrinal beliefs of the church. Nowadays, people get carried away with the hype of worship, making music the center of their experience, when it is the solid "meat," the Word of God that feeds the soul. The Psalmist David declared "Your word *is* a lamp to my feet and a light to my path" (Psalm 119:105). He further stated that "The entrance of Your words gives light; It gives understanding to the simple (Vs. 130). There is no substitute for the proper understanding of the Bible. A periodic expose and affirmation of doctrinal beliefs can only be a positive benefit for the entire church.

I do a doctrinal series on our fundamental beliefs every other year over the course of two quarters. It has a uniting effect and there is the added benefit of a spiritual renewal among the membership. This also answers the questions members may be harboring but never felt comfortable asking. I should point out too that I do not preach this series. I teach it as a Bible study series to make it interactive and user-friendly for the members. They are able to ask their questions and get immediate feedback, thus clarifying their understanding of the tenets of our faith.

A strong emphasis on the church's doctrinal beliefs helps members to be grounded in the Word of God, but to also renew their commitment to their local church. A clearer sense of knowing increases the sense of belonging. The role of the church in society is reinforced, and members who understand that tend to be more appreciative of the need to rightly represent both the church and the Lord to society.

Teach the Facts and Value of Church Policy

Throughout my earlier ministry, I noticed that most of the really vocal members who objected to what I was doing in terms of leading the church were individuals who did not appear to know what they were opposing. In quite a few cases, people opposed me doing my job as clearly outlined in the Church Manual. I began paying close attention to this phenomenon. Sure enough, I discovered, by asking questions, that most members did not own a copy of the current edition of the Manual.

The Church Manual, or the Constitution and Bylaws as used by some faith communions, plays a very important role in the efficient running of the church. The pastor should know church policy backward and forward. It is incredible how many pastors do not have a comprehensive grasp of essential policy information... that they are paid to know and utilize in their work! In my experience as a counselor to many pastors who seek my advice about how to handle certain challenges, I have seen that in many cases, it is a lack of knowledge of church policy that got them in trouble with the saints. No pastor can afford to be less knowledgeable of church policy than the members.

The Seventh-day Adventist Church Manual provides, among other things: vital information about local church and denominational structure, and the relationship between the various administrative levels of the Church; the role of pastors and other denominational employees, especially as it relates to the local church; how churches are established and disbanded; how a person becomes a member of the church and why and how membership may be withdrawn or otherwise changed; the causes and procedures of church discipline; qualifications for holding church office and what constitutes the ministry responsibilities of each office; how to conduct local church elections, and; summary statements on our fundamental beliefs.

The Manual is a vital tool, a guide for some things (such as what offices are to be filled during elections), but the absolute rule for others (church discipline and doctrinal beliefs). In the former, the local church enjoys a limited degree of autonomy, whereas in the latter, the local church has no autonomy whatsoever, since it is only in General Conference Session that doctrinal statements can be formulated or amended.

As in the case of doing a doctrinal teaching series, I also conduct a church policy teaching series every two years. The Bible and the Church Manual are the text books for this series. I prepare a study guide for the Manual, which the members use to prepare each week's teaching session for the mid-week service, and we have great discussions about the nature and work of the church. It is a special joy each time that I do the church policy series, to hear the testimonies of the saints, as they share how by actually doing a systematic study of the Manual, they better know, understand, and appreciate why and how things are done in the church.

Some view church policies as hindrances, but rightly understood, policies clarify what, who, when, why, and how things get done. Policy is intended to safeguard the church, and should therefore be followed (within the intended context). This is important, because some make the mistake of elevating policy to the level of Scripture. This is sometimes the catalyst for conflict in the church! The study of policy can be a tremendous benefit in every church, but especially where there is church conflict. Complaints about what the pastor does, and how he or she does it, are a leading cause of tension and conflict in many churches. If only more people would acquire a copy of the church's policy manual or Constitution, and spend the time learning about what their pastors went to school for years to prepare for. And the pastor who cherishes the people under his care should not short-change the church by failing to be an informed leader.

The Role of Appropriate Church Discipline

Sadly, there are times when the church must express its displeasure (which is actually the displeasure of God) in the form of discipline because of a member's choices. Notice how I said that: The church does not initiate disciplinary action against members, but rather responds to members' choices that may necessitate biblically mandated disciplinary remedies to particular conduct and sin.

One of the biggest mistakes in most churches is a high tolerance for sin and in particular, people who do not care about "the wellbeing and prosperity of the church." These are the ones who don't mind tearing down the church with openly sinful conduct that undermines the church's missional effectiveness. Among the greatest of these are those who sow discord among brethren. God has declared His own sentiments about destroyers of churches:

> These six things the Lord hates, Yes, seven are an abomination to Him: A proud look, A lying tongue, Hands that shed innocent blood, A heart that devises wicked plans, Feet that are swift in running to evil, A false witness who speaks lies, And one who sows discord among brethren (Proverbs 6:16-19).

The thing that I find interesting, and very sad, is the fact that God has expressed such strong disgust at those who intentionally seek to divide the church, and yet the church itself acts as if this behavior is tolerable or at least unpunishable. I have personally witnessed the consequences of what can happen to a congregation of mostly innocent people when rogue elements are allowed to freely exist and operate among the sheep. It is not pretty! In one pastorate, the LORD rebuked me for being overly longsuffering with the wolves, while they consumed the sheep... in plain sight. I have vowed never to do that again. God had to show me that He did not call me to the ministry to protect wolves, but the sheep, even when the sheep believe that the wolves (masquerading as sheep) are actually saints.

Insist on Excellence, Tolerate Nothing Less!

One dictionary defines excellence as "the quality of being outstanding or extremely good." My first observation is that excellence pertains to "quality." Imagine a church where the members, especially the pastor, officers and ministry leaders make the personal and collective decision to make the "quality" of their ministry and the worship services their highest priority. They are intentional about creating a culture of being outstanding or extremely good at what they do. Just try to envision the many ways in which your own church would be immediately transformed.

As a pastor, it is my responsibility to educate, train, motivate, and hold myself, our church officers, and the entire membership to a high standard of excellence in all that we do for God. I am not advocating that we strive for perfection, but that we purpose in our hearts to do the best that we can do through the baptism of the Holy Spirit, commensurate with the spiritual gift with which we have been entrusted to build up the kingdom of God.

There is no good reason why the church bulletin cannot be beautiful, neat, and free of misspelled words. Nothing can justify dried up plants on the stage in the sanctuary. It is better to have silk plants than to display the evidence of lack of interest in making the worship space appealing. Why can't the music coordinator and the various choir leaders and musicians set aside time to properly prepare for the worship services? It would really be great if the deacons would be consistent about cutting the grass… and make sure to do the edging too. How about the folks in the children's division actually preparing appealing programs that the kids are excited about? The church board meetings do not have to be acrimonious, because members understand that we are on the same team.

Imagine a church where guests are not asked to stand and introduce themselves. Instead, the ushers insure that guests fill out the guest registration cards, and those cards are handed to the person tasked with doing the welcome. That person introduces all guests by name, and the members sitting in front, behind, and on both sides of all guests extend a friendly smile and handshake while introducing themselves. That would make a huge difference in our churches, wouldn't it?

I advise my members that I am not authorized to accept anything less than excellence. Remember my operating principle – "if you can't do it at your job, you won't be allowed to do it here." Church members need to be held to a higher standard. I get that they are volunteers, but it works for me... primarily because my members understand that it is for the glory of God. Pastors need to raise the stakes, and the people will follow. True, some will balk at first (thank God for church elections), but most will be grateful for the transformation you inspire by being forward thinking, gracious and firm in your approach to church leadership.

My recommendation is that church leaders need not be afraid to introduce necessary change. The key is to inform, educate, inspire, motivate, and for heaven's sake, lead. As long as you lead with love and grace, people will come along for the journey. If they lash out at you, don't worry about it. That is your opportunity to be reminded of God's promise to His leaders. He says, "Have I not commanded you? Be strong and of good courage; do not be afraid, nor be dismayed, for the Lord your God *is* with you wherever you go" (Joshua 1:9). Set high expectations of your team. They will rise to the challenge.

Professional Congregational Conflict Resolution Training

Through my consulting service CLASS Act Seminars, LLC, I offer and conduct great programs for congregations. I focus on the pastor-elder team, church board orientation, and congregational conflict training. For churches in serious crisis, I offer mediation services as a Registered Neutral (Licensed Mediator). Obviously, I am unable to do work for every imaginable church. I recommend utilizing a trained conflict professional to help your church heal.

Create a Culture of Accountability

In order to transition a church from holy hell to hallelujah again, a fresh, new climate of order must be ushered in. No longer can the church be held hostage by unruly elements. No longer should the innocents be made to suffer at the hands of those who sow discord. It is time to create a culture of accountability. Through sermons, town hall meetings, and other opportunities to inform and inspire the people, the pastor must make a stand and begin a sustained effort of raising the collective conscience of the membership to be their brother's keeper in provoking one another to righteousness.

The pastor has to rise to the occasion and lead reforms that will be unpopular for those who are up to no good. In my pastorates, I make it clear that I am not tolerating any kind of outburst against any member, in any meeting or elsewhere. I make it abundantly clear that no member will disrespect me (remember, I have been abused in two churches in my earlier ministry). I lay out the consequences. They understand that I am not speaking idle words, because they have seen me take action against those who dare to violate the high standard of mutual respect that I have said will prevail in the church. It is high time that the church stops being the place where the worst kinds of behaviors are excused, justified, accepted and "forgiven" by the people who are not the ones who have to suffer the pain of some unconverted person's satanic wrath.

It is to be understood that every member, including me as pastor, is personally responsible for our attitudes, words, and conduct. No exceptions. The church is not a plaything; it is the body of Christ. Real people are getting really hurt in too many of our churches while church leaders sit on our hands and worry about who will get mad and leave when we take a stand. Enough is enough.

Every church needs two Christians who have the holy boldness needed to change the church. Only two courageous Christians... one to move the motion, and the other to second the motion to take action against those people who mean the church no good. Accountability is absolutely needed and necessary. Let's do it.

Transition to a Missional Focus

We have examined quite a bit of information in these steps that I have recommended to transition a conflicted church. This final step is just as crucial as the others. It is common knowledge that the devil finds work for idle hands. Everything that we have discussed in this chapter up to this point is intended to move the church toward this point. This is the culmination of all our efforts... transitioning to a missional focus.

It was the departure from a missional emphasis that caused the church to become distracted in the first place. Much has happened among the people. There is hurt, anger, discouragement, doubt, disillusionment, and many other negative feelings. Some members have probably left, never to ever return. Some will come back after a while, when they hear of the healing and transformation that has taken place.

The disciples were constantly at variance with each other, until they went into the upper room and found out that it was never about them. This realization brought a sense of shame and a redirected purpose of heart. Finally, when they were with one accord, the Holy Spirit was poured out on them in copious showers and tremendous power to carry on the missional purpose of the church. In one day, three thousand souls were added to the church. That is the result of a missional focus! Imagine this happening at your church.

This step requires that we make grand plans (hopefully, we included this in the strategic plan) for outreach and evangelism. Soul winning will begin to occur when the church begins to simmer down and heal, but more will be accomplished when intentional plans are laid to enlarge the kingdom of God. Surely, that is something that God will be excited about, to the extent that He will not sit on the sidelines as a spectator. No, He will pour out His power and people will begin to be saved in your community through your church!

Hallelujah Again!

I have had the privilege of seeing two very conflicted congregations through the transformation process. The process is very hard work. There are lonely days and sleepless nights. There are times when you question the return on investment of your nerves, guts, and will. It is human to feel the stress when those who have been holding down a church for years and years are pushing back at you, and you don't have the luxury of using the tactics of abuse, slander, and acrimony that they resort to in order to remain in control of the church you are there to rescue from their deadly grasp.

The one thing that keeps you going is the knowledge that God is with you. He has promised success if we are faithful. The task appears impossible at times, but God is able. The first church took three-and-a-half years to turn around. It was brutal, but I survived and lived to draw upon the lessons that I still lean on to this day. Those lessons prepared me to do successful conflict ministry and transition the next church. This church was more brutal than the first, but I was equal to the task. God had prepared me well.

My family was badly hurt by this church, and I had to learn in that assignment that it was not alright to do nothing when I clearly saw the unconverted class deliberately driving people out of the church (they took them home and fed them poison for potluck after service and I watched then do it for nearly a year before taking action even though some who were victimized by the practice reported to me and confirmed what I already knew). It took four-and-a-half years, but that church finally turned. It was while serving there that I earned my doctoral degree with a concentration and specialization in congregational conflict resolution training.

That church will never again be what it was when I arrived there, when I was the seventh pastor in its twenty-three years of existence on the day of my installation. I installed new local leadership, implemented a culture of accountability and many of the steps that I have shared in this chapter, and the rest is history. Truly, in these two churches, the saints can testify that they were delivered from holy hell to hallelujah again!

Group Discussion

1. How important is leadership in the transition process?

2. Share your views of the use of the church election to help in the transformation process of the church.

3. Craft a mission statement for the "Anywhere But Here Community Church"

4. Why is the church manual important to church administration and for helping a congregation to regain a missional focus?

5. Talk about the ramifications of creating a culture of accountability in the "Anywhere But Here Community Church"

Reflection Questions

1. Ministerial student - Are you ready for pastoral ministry?

2. Conference administrator – What can you do to provide better training for your pastors to take on the rigors of transitioning churches?

3. Pastor – How willing are you to invest resources in providing professional training and equipping to your local leaders and the congregation?

4. College professor – How can you better prepare your ministerial students for the real world of pastoral ministry?

PART FOUR

HEALING THE WOUNDS: ANOTHER LOOK AT REPENTANCE, FORGIVENESS & RECONCILIATION

CHAPTER 11

The Role and Responsibility of the Offended in Conflict Resolution

Offended – One harmed by the injurious attitudes, actions or words of another.

Duty of the Offended

Typical (ineffective) Responses of the Offended

- Passive Withdrawal - Silence, sulking, coldness, etc.

- Triangulation - Telling third parties about the matter without first seeking to resolve it with the offender

- Desire for Revenge – Harboring the hurt, which then ripens into malice (evil intent or desire to do harm)

- Aggressive Counter-Attack – Offended is in fight mode; the use of malicious spoken or written words and taking action to get even with (hurt) the offender

- Unforgiveness - Even after the offender has repented

What God Requires of the Offended

- Acknowledge the issue and the hurt that's in your own heart. Do not secretly hold a matter against another that he does not know you're hurting over – Leviticus 19:17(a)

- Address the problem to the offender (there are very important reasons for this, including clarifying the issue, preventing the spreading of misperceptions, and promoting a positive outcome) – Matt. 18:15

- The purpose of first speaking with the offender alone is to seek to resolve the dispute at the lowest level possible and with the fewest number of people necessary. Most disputes would be resolved at this level if this rule were diligently carried out. This is why it is critical that when someone brings a matter to you about a difficulty with another, the first words out of a serious Christian's mouth should be, "Have you discussed this matter with him or her (the party against whom the complaint is being made to you)?" This question will stop ninety percent of all discussions about someone behind their back immediately. Refer the individual to the biblical rule and counsel them to follow the protocol in good faith, trusting that God will honor their obedience to His Word.

- Forgive the repentant offender (Unforgiveness hinders reconciliation) – Luke 17:3, 4; Matt. 18:21-35

  Whatever the character of the offense, this does not change the plan that God has made for the settlement of misunderstandings and personal injuries. Speaking alone and in the spirit of Christ to the one who is in fault will often remove the difficulty. Go to the erring one, with a heart filled with Christ's love and sympathy, and seek to adjust the matter. Reason with him calmly and quietly. Let no angry words escape your lips. Speak in a way that will appeal to his better judgment. Remember the words: "He which converteth the sinner from the error of his way shall save a soul from death, and shall hide a multitude of sins" (James 5:20).[1]

Notes

1. White, *Testimonies for the Church*, 7:261.

CHAPTER 12

The Role and Responsibility of the Offender

Offender – One who causes harm to another through attitudes, actions or words; an abuser or attacker.

Duty of the Offended

Typical (and ineffective) Responses of Offenders

- Denial or justification of wrongdoing, hence, no repentance or apology for wrong done

- Demanding forgiveness, acceptance or reconciliation without any acknowledgement of, remorse for, or cessation of wrongdoing (usually done by talking about the perceived "unforgiveness" of the offended)

- Blaming the victim for the offense (common in cases of domestic abuse, but not limited to that setting)

- Insincere 'apology' – "If I offended you, I am sorry"

- Continuation or escalation of the offensive behavior

What God Requires of the Offender

- Acknowledge (confess) the wrong done and the hurt caused – James 5:16

- Repentance (discontinue the offence) – Luke 17:3, 4

- Restore whatever was stolen from the offended

  ✓ Dignity (one's sense of self-esteem)

  ✓ Reputation (how a person is viewed)

  ✓ Influence (a person's ability to have a positive impact on others)

  ✓ Financial Restitution (in severe cases of loss; awarded in lawsuits)

- Apology – private or public (depending on the original forum in which the offence was given)

One of the most critical aspects of biblical conflict resolution is the responsibility of the offending party, both to the offended party and to God. Of this responsibility, Poirier writes, "If we are ever to witness true reconciliation, the peacemaking process must begin with confession."[1] Poirier continues by stressing that in addition to confessing sins to God, the offending parties also confess to one another regarding sinful words, attitudes, and actions. In this exhortation, he specifically shows how a confession should be done, using the "Seven A's of Confession" which include: (1) Address everyone involved; (2) Avoid if, but, and maybe; (3) Admit specifically; (4) Accept the consequences; (5) Alter your behavior; (6) Ask forgiveness; and (7) Allow time for the offended party to forgive.[2] On the last note, Poirier further states,

> Assuming the person we are counseling has made a good confession of sin, it remains incumbent upon us as peacemaking pastors to help the one confessing a sin to distinguish the difference between God's immediate response to a confession made and the various reasons why the one who has been offended may be slow to respond.[3]

Poirier additionally explains, "If I confess my sin to a brother, I cannot and should not be the one who demands he forgive me. Before God, it is my responsibility to confess my sin, while it is his responsibility to forgive."[4] I have seen many make this very mistake, resulting in worsened conflict when the offender has "confessed" their sin against the offended, and then started a campaign of demanding forgiveness. This is usually done by telling others or by telling the offended party how unforgiving they are. It is a guilt trip designed to pacify the guilty conscience of an offender who has not truly confessed or repented. This is an attempt to control the emotions of the hurt party, and it results in greater emotional harm and anger, further alienating the offended person.

Even though Matt 18:15-20 is clearly the will of God as articulated by Jesus, it is also true that people find it hard to come to a solution to their particular conflict or challenge. This is "because we are fallen people who do not always think alike, and sometimes we do not know how to come to resolution."[5]

As we reflect on and rejoice in the gospel of Christ . . . we can let go of our illusion of self-righteousness, honestly examine ourselves, and find freedom from guilt and sin by admitting our wrongs . . . repair any harm we have caused to others and to be reconciled to those we have offended."[6]

It takes mutual commitment, in addition to cooperation with all parties to conflict and faithful obedience to the Word of God, for true resolution to be achieved among feuding parties. One party cannot successfully conclude conflict. The centrality of the Cross is a power for transforming the human heart from a heart of stone to a heart of flesh so that reconciliation is made possible.

What About the Unrepentant Offender?

- Unfortunately, ego and pride often prevent offenders from acknowledging that they have wronged others, even when there's no question about it (most of the times we know when we are wrong)

- For unrepentant offenders, see Matthew 18:16, 17

- The offended can (and often must choose) to forgive the offender, even in the absence of an apology

- Unrepentant offenders hinder reconciliation

- What does Luke 23:34 mean?

  The apostle says, "Confess your faults one to another, and pray one for another, that ye may be healed." James 5:16. Confess your sins to God, who only can forgive them, and your faults to one another. If you have given offense to your friend or neighbor, you are to acknowledge your wrong, and it is his duty freely to forgive you. Then you are to seek the forgiveness of God, because the brother you have wounded is the property of God, and in injuring him you sinned against his Creator and Redeemer. The case is brought before the only true Mediator, our great High Priest, who "was in all points tempted like as we are, yet without sin," and who is "touched with the feeling of our infirmities," and is able to cleanse from every stain of iniquity. Hebrews 4:15.[7]

Notes

1. Poirier, *The Peace Making Pastor*, 113.

2. Ibid., 118-131.

3. Ibid., 129.

4. Ibid., 130.

5. Chris Brauns, *Unpacking Forgiveness: Biblical Answers for Complex Questions and Deep Wounds* (Wheaton, IL: Crossway, 2008), 180.

6. Sande, *The Peace Maker*, 117.

7. Ellen G. White, *Steps to Christ* (1892; repr., Mountain View, CA: Pacific Press, 1956), 37.

CHAPTER 13

The Role and Responsibility of the Observer

Observer – Third party who has firsthand knowledge of wrongdoing, or one who is made aware of alleged wrong-doing through the testimony of other witnesses (which may include the testimony of the offended and offender); One who is called upon to adjudicate or to be a juror in a dispute or conflict.

All human beings play the role of the offended, the offender and the observer from time to time.

Typical (very negative) Responses of Observers

- Bystander Apathy – Avoidance, disengagement, indifference, disregard for the suffering of the abused

- Fear – Public silence, but private 'support' for the abused

- Partiality – Unfair judgment: Taking sides with the offender, often due to a personal friendship, family relationship or bribery (material or otherwise)

- Mob Enchantment – Caught up in the demonically induced emotional frenzy against the innocent (Num. 16:1-50; Matt. 27:15-26)

- Constructive observer intervention in congregational conflict is extremely rare, as compared to the responses above

The Duty of Observers in Conflict Resolution

- Scripture addresses the role of observers of conflict more than it addresses the role of the parties who are directly involved! Observers may be: Family members, friends, eyewitnesses, judges, co-workers, church members, neighbors, members of a jury, leaders, supervisors, passersby, etc.

- In matters that are formally or informally adjudicated, it is the observer who judges (decides innocence or guilt, right or wrong)

God Requires Righteous Judgment

- John 7:24 – Don't judge based on their faces!

- Prov. 24:23-25 – It's not good to show partiality

- Lev. 19:15 – Judge your neighbor fairly, impartially

- Deut. 1:9-17 – "Don't be partial… don't be afraid of anyone, for judgment belongs to God…"

- Deut. 16:18-20 – "do not pervert [twist] others' words…in judgment"

- Prov. 17:15 – The partial [unfair] observer and the offender are both an abomination to God!

- Exodus 23:1-9 – Don't circulate a false report…bribe

Observers to conflict have more responsibility than is generally realized. This is especially true when dealing with disputes in the church, seeing that Paul's admonition plainly states:

> Dare any of you, having a matter against another, go to law before the unrighteous, and not before the saints? Do you not know that the saints will judge the world? And if the world will be judged by you, are you unworthy to judge the smallest matters? Do you not know that we shall judge angels? How much more, things that pertain to this life? If then you have judgments concerning things pertaining to this life, do you appoint those who are least esteemed by the church to judge? I say this to your shame. Is it so, that there is not a wise man among you, not even one, who will be able to judge between his brethren? But brother goes to law against brother, and that before unbelievers! Now therefore, it is already an utter failure for you that you go to law against one another. Why do you not rather accept wrong? Why do you not rather let yourselves be cheated? 1 Corinthians 6:1-7.

The church has a very important role in dealing with disputes among its members. The way to deal with the reality of conflict is not to ignore the problem, but to equip, train, and organize the church for conflict ministry. This begins with a rightly trained leadership team comprising the pastor and elders of the church, the pastoral staff.

The church also has a responsibility to teach its members how to deal with conflict in all other aspects of their lives, including family issues, problems on their jobs, and dealing with the personal struggles of emotional and spiritual immaturity. All of these realities are the business of the church. It may be that the church's failure (due to lack of sensitivity or training) has contributed to some of the very issues we have examined in this book. Nonetheless, we can thank God for giving us this training program to bring greater awareness and more understanding to the issue of congregational conflict.

PART FIVE

CONFLICT MINISTRY AWARENESS & TRAINING FOR MINISTERIAL STUDENTS, PASTORS, AND DENOMINATIONAL LEADERS

CHAPTER 14

Pastors and Elders as Conflict Ministers

Elders and Congregational Conflict

The Jethro Plan (Exodus 18) for conflict ministry is the genesis of a codified ministry paradigm including elders of the people. The context was the wisdom of Jethro in sensing that Moses could not single-handedly judge the cases of all the people. Elders, by divine design, are burden bearers and problem solvers. That is their primary role. When we compare what elders do today and what they did in the days of Moses, we get a sense of why conflict seems to be overwhelming for the church. There is almost no one that is doing specialized conflict ministry! Not even the pastors.

In Deuteronomy 1:9-18, Moses said:

> And I spoke to you at that time, saying: 'I alone am not able to bear you. The Lord your God has multiplied you, and here you are today, as the stars of heaven in multitude. May the Lord God of your fathers make you

a thousand times more numerous than you are, and bless you as He has promised you! How can I alone bear your problems and your burdens and your complaints? Choose wise, understanding, and knowledgeable men from among your tribes, and I will make them heads over you.' And you answered me and said, 'The thing which you have told us to do is good.' So I took the heads of your tribes, wise and knowledgeable men, and made them heads over you, leaders of thousands, leaders of hundreds, leaders of fifties, leaders of tens, and officers for your tribes. "Then I commanded your judges at that time, saying, 'Hear the cases between your brethren, and judge righteously between a man and his brother or the stranger who is with him. You shall not show partiality in judgment; you shall hear the small as well as the great; you shall not be afraid in any man's presence, for the judgment is God's. The case that is too hard for you, bring to me, and I will hear it.' And I commanded you at that time all the things which you should do.

Pastors are elders too (overseers of the flock of God). Peter identified himself as an elder (1 Peter 5:1). Elders are called to work together to protect the flock from the devourer. Satan unsettles the church members through his scattering influence and seeks to destroy their confidence in God. Pastors and elders must be vigilant to preserve that which God has entrusted to our care.

This book has focused considerable attention on the seriousness of congregational conflict and given numerous suggestions about how we can both prevent and reverse the effects of conflict to the church. I have advocated very strongly for pastors and elders to be trained and to work closely to help members deal with conflict. But what about the practical steps to accomplishing this goal?

The Pastor's Role in Conflict Training

- Teach the people how to live – Exodus 18:19, 20

- Appoint carefully selected Elders – Vs. 21 (see also 1 Timothy 3:1-7 and Titus 1:5-9)

- Enlist the assistance and expertise of a qualified consultant or trainer

- Model the principles of conflict ministry

- Implement and practice mutual accountability for biblical conflict resolution among the pastoral staff

The Elder's Role in Conflict Training

- Assist and support the pastor in teaching the people how to live – Exodus 18:19, 20

- Model the principles of biblical conflict resolution in how you relate to other elders and your pastor

- Hold yourself and your own household to God's high standard of peace and harmony in the Church

- Insure that your own conduct is exemplary and be prepared to adjust if it is not

Elders Should Avoid Preventable Conflict with the Pastor

- The Elder's Responsibility in fostering an atmosphere of peace among the pastoral staff and among the congregation

- Please refer to Exhibit B in the Appendix for the Elder's Ten Commandments

How Elders Can Prevent and Resolve Conflict with Their Pastor

- Personally talk with your pastor about your concerns

- Don't abandon/ambush the pastor in meetings

- Be especially careful not to misuse the influence that comes with your office to undermine the pastor's influence with the people

- Disagree with your pastor respectfully, in the proper forum and in the right tone

- Don't view your pastor as an enemy or an outsider. That is a terrible mistake that's too often made. Your pastor is a Christian, and a member the Church like everyone else

- Difference of opinion is a given; conflict is a choice! Choose to handle matters in a Christ-like manner. Choose to be non-judgmental and non-confrontational.

- Don't expect to be trusted after you've undermined your pastor with the members!

- Learn to disagree without being disagreeable!

"And we urge you, brethren, to recognize those who labor among you, and are over you in the Lord and admonish you, And to esteem them very highly in love for their work's sake. Be at peace among yourselves" (1 Thessalonians 5:12, 13).

> Remember those who rule over you, who have spoken the word of God to you, whose faith follow, considering the outcome of their conduct... Obey those who rule over you, and be submissive, for they watch out for your souls, as those who must give account. Let them do so with joy and not with grief, for that would be unprofitable for you (Hebrews 13:7, 17).

When Your Pastor Is at Fault

The Elder has a responsibility in helping the pastor to be a better and more effective servant of God.

What to Do When the Pastor Errs?

- Pastors do make mistakes sometimes, and sometimes do wrong things, say wrong things, leave an undesirable impression.

- Sometimes, ministry plans don't work out as expected. Pastors have flaws as do members...

- Pastors are human beings. We have strengths, weaknesses, limitations and flaws, just like... you. Sometimes we don't think of pastors as humans...

Proper Steps to Take

- Don't rush to call the conference!

- Be very slow to react based upon your feelings. I read a wonderful statement online recently. It said: "Don't make permanent decisions in the heat of your temporary anger."

- The first thing you should do is pray about the matter.

- After you pray, go to your pastor.

Take It Slow... Breathe... Clarify... Be Open

- Probably the majority of church problems are based on "perceptions" that were not clarified!

- Don't rush to discuss your feelings with other elders or members of the church family. First, clarify your feelings, your motive, and the reason for your concern. Make sure you understand what your pastor is doing, why he or she is going in the direction that you're concerned about.

- The absolutely best way to truly understand your pastor's direction and intention is to have a personal talk with him or her!

- Make an appointment to sit down and reason together. Don't make the excuse that your pastor doesn't listen to anyone!

- Be careful not to misrepresent your pastor...

- Be willing to follow the process of gaining understanding. It's possible your views are wrong!

Is Your Pastor's Path "Wrong" or Different?

- Also, be especially careful before you label your pastor's course of action as "wrong".

- Is it actually wrong, or is it just different from what you're accustomed to... different from how you've always done it? Being wrong and being different are not synonymous. Don't falsely accuse your pastor of wrong-doing! People are listening to what you say. This has consequences for your pastor's influence and his or her ability to lead.

Essential Core Values

- Elders should not be quarrelsome people – 1 Timothy 3:3 "not violent, not greedy for money, but gentle, not quarrelsome, not covetous."

- Teamwork is crucial. Do your part well. Work more and talk less. Don't make a habit of finding fault with your teammates.

- Complaining does not build up the church. Elders should co-operate and collaborate.

How Elders Can Help Members as Conflict Ministers

The Elder has a great responsibility in helping every member to be a peacemaker.

Peacemaking Elders:

- Hold members accountable to Matthew 18:15-20

- Do not accept a bad report from anyone against another party without verifying that the complainant has followed Matthew 18

- Correct or rebuke members who enlist their assistance in speaking against the pastor or other elders

- Diligently seek to guide conflicting parties to resolution and reconciliation before involving the pastor

- Are faithful to the Word of God

CHAPTER 15

From Conflict Misery to Conflict Ministry

The information presented in this chapter is by no means exhaustive as it relates to the subject under consideration, and there might be alternate views and approaches to the problem being addressed which may be as valid as those presented here. I acknowledge the humanity of pastors; men and women who possess strengths, weaknesses, limitations and flaws, not unlike the members we lead. The purpose of this particular section is to equip and encourage pastors toward a more effective ministry of reconciliation in the local church. This information will not necessarily result in the resolution of every problem in any church, nor will it exempt pastors or congregations from experiencing conflict in the future.

Statement of Affirmation

It is the position of CLASS Act Seminars (Dr. Everton A. Ennis) that while pastors are imperfect human beings, the vast majority of pastors are doing a great job in their churches, and that most congregational conflict is not in fact caused by the pastor. It is also the position of CLASS Act Seminars that ministry "success" is best defined as faithfulness to God and His Church, in the context of a particular pastor's assigned local congregation, and without regard to any comparison with another pastor's ministry or the circumstances existing in any other congregation.

As seen earlier in this book, one of the problems in dealing with conflict is that there is no unified working definition of conflict!

Can all conflict be prevented by the pastor?

There are many different possible causes of conflict. No pastor can control what members do or how members behave. In my dissertation, I came up with a categorization of seven types of causes of congregational conflict, drawn from biblical accounts of conflict. Most conflicts involving pastors are NOT caused by pastors, but by church members' reactions to the pastor's leadership. Pastors can learn how to mitigate against some conflict, but it is unreasonable to charge any pastor with the sole responsibility for church conflict. Often, in our conclusions, we fail to take into account the biblical injunction, "If it be possible, as much as lieth in you, live peaceably with all men." – Rom. 12:18

The Reality of Conflict: As Long as There's a Devil!

1. Moses is described as the meekest man who ever lived, and yet he was subjected to such inhumane treatment as the leader of Israel.

2. Nehemiah's sole focus was the restoration of Jerusalem and the Temple, yet he was persistently set upon by would-be detractors. "I am doing a great work; I will not come down..."

3. Jesus is perfect and is the Prince of Peace! Yet, He was relentlessly criticized, persecuted and ultimately killed... not for doing anything wrong, but for doing some things differently!

4. Matthew 5:9 – Peacemakers shall be called sons of God.

5. Matthew 5:10-12 – You will be persecuted, as were the prophets!

Conflict "conclusion" is an emerging focus in the conflict resolution and mediation field.

1. Reconciliation is the divine ideal, but it takes all sides doing their biblical part to make this happen.

2. The biggest problem in conflict resolution in the church is not the lack of forgiveness, but a lack of repentance (acknowledging and apologizing for wrong done)!

Can the Conflicts in Your Church be Resolved?

Most of them can be! Here are some ideas how…

1. Christ-centered preaching: Focus more on grace and righteousness by faith; too many of our members are cranky and critical because they don't have the peace of God reigning in their hearts.

2. Preach and teach on godly relationships, and call sin by its right name!

3. Get qualified help – qualified 3rd party intervention is often helpful!

4. Church elections need to be better managed!

5. Teach the elders to be burden bearers and problem solvers!

6. We are called to the "ministry of reconciliation." Be a good example to the church in how to prevent and resolve conflict.

Therefore, if anyone is in Christ, he is a new creation; old things have passed away; behold, all things have become new. Now all things are of God, who has reconciled us to Himself through Jesus Christ, and has given us the ministry of reconciliation, that is, that God was in Christ reconciling the world to Himself, not imputing their trespasses to them, and has committed to us the word of reconciliation. Now then, we are ambassadors for Christ, as though God were pleading through us: we implore you on Christ's behalf, be reconciled to God. For He made Him who knew no sin to be sin for us, that we might become the righteousness of God in Him (2 Corinthians 5:17-21).

CHAPTER 16

The Role of Denominational Leadership and the Ministerial Training Curriculum in Effective Conflict Ministry

Conflict is inevitable and also potentially destructive if not addressed and concluded correctly. The fact of the matter is that church members and pastors generally do not have the natural desire or ability to remedy conflict or potential conflict. This means that people need to be taught, equipped for the task. This task is one that confronts us each and every day in varying forms. How well we relate to it will be informed by our level of exposure to methodologies that are geared toward helping us to not be afraid of conflict, but to intelligently and systematically address and conclude the threat of damage with the hopeful result of reconciliation.

Conflict does not have to automatically mean the end of relationships. Christ's purpose for the conflict resolution protocol outlined in Matthew 18:15-20 and Luke 17:3, 4 is the reconciliation of disputing parties. It should be understood that this is not always possible, as the offended and the offender both have to be willing to allow for that to happen. The church represents the redemptive and healing grace of God, and as such, should do all in its power to educate its members on how to prevent and recover from conflict.

Conflicted churches can recover and become healthy again, given skilled leadership is provided. I have had the blessing to experience the transition of two congregations from holy hell to hallelujah again. It is a triumphant feeling, one that reinforces the goodness and power of God to heal. This type of conflict ministry calls for more emphasis to be placed on how pastors are trained. More pastors would benefit greatly, and so would the congregations they lead, if they were properly trained in the art of conflict ministry.

Conflict ministry as it relates to the transition of severely damaged churches is probably not for everyone, even though at the minimum, every pastor should be equipped to handle the more typical church issues. Perhaps the work that I have been able to do is more of a specialty, in the way that some medical doctors branch out into a specialized area of medicine. Congregational transitioning requires a certain type of personality, and maybe even a certain quality of local leadership. One thing is sure – no one person can do this work.

Many denominational leaders do not appear to have the level of appreciation for the complexities of congregational conflict that would promote a change from the typical denominational reaction of moving the pastor when there are several calls from church members about conflict. Most church conflicts originate among the laity, not the clergy. Leadership has always been subjected to criticism, abuse, and general unfair evaluations. While pastors are not perfect, it is not productive to simply view the transfer of the pastor as the solution to the church's woes. In fact, in the typical conflicted congregation, the record will show (if it is actually looked at) that several pastors have faced the same issues in that church. And it is usually the same members who are involved in the problems, regardless of who the pastor is or was.

A different, more intelligent approach is needed when the members call the conference headquarters to complain about their pastor. The downside to this scenario is that the goodly folks who work in the regional headquarters are usually themselves ill-equipped and mostly untrained to handle congregational conflict! Yet, they (by virtue of their office) get to make decisions to move pastors, and usually resort to that nuclear option too quickly – again, because they don't really know how to handle the real problems in the church.

In most cases of congregational conflict, the real problem is not the pastor. Members project their issues onto whoever the pastor is. If the conference takes a bit of time to send a new pastor, the interim pastor (usually a retired pastor) or the head elder that is holding it down, becomes the target for complaints and murmuring. It never fails. Yet, church leaders continue to sacrifice good pastors, men and women, due to their own inability to rein in the people who are troubling the church.

My Final Recommendations and Conclusion

Having experienced both personal and professional growth in knowledge, understanding, and response to congregational conflict, I deem it a blessing to have gone on the remarkable academic journey toward a doctoral degree and learning how to deal more effectively with this ever-present reality that has destroyed many homes, lives, and congregations. There is no question that this has been a most rewarding learning experience for me. I have acquired much knowledge, enough to know that there is yet so much more for me to learn. Indeed, my scholarly appetite has been aroused to a new level of inquiry. I would recommend that more pastors avail themselves of the opportunity to improve their personal effectiveness in conflict ministry, but also to strengthen our colleagues who have not had that privilege and are in need of our helping hand and our prayers.

The personal and pastoral benefits which have already resulted in significant changes in my life and my ministry are profound. This reality affords me the humbling privilege of making the following recommendations about congregational conflict resolution training:

1. That local conferences or other denominational entities make congregational conflict resolution training for pastors a priority, recognizing the need to move away from the traditional and highly unproductive tendency of moving pastors when there is major conflict in the churches, seeing that churches do not generally improve as a result, and not to mention the stigma that follows the pastor who is perceived to have failed.

2. That Ministerial Directors be required to undergo specialized training in the area of congregational conflict resolution, in order to better serve and support the pastors in their fields. This is a critical need, one that would serve as an important step in the move away from merely resorting to moving the pastor when church members write or call the conference office to complain about their leader.

3. That a study be done to seek to determine what percentage of church conflict is actually caused by the pastor, versus the percentage of conflicts that were embedded in the church history and culture before the current pastors were installed, and versus the amount which occurred during the pastors' tenures.

4. That a profile of every church be compiled and kept on record at every conference office. This would be based upon the

observations of pastors who have served the congregations, as well as conference office personnel who have interacted with the congregations over the years, especially in the area of conflict. This profile could greatly assist conference leaders in decision making when the time comes to send a new pastor, or when the decision must be made to take a stand by insisting that a pastor will not be moved based on the outcry of the people, given the conflicted history of the church.

It has been my privilege to share this book with you. May the grace of God be upon you, your ministry, and your congregation as you implement those principles of this book that apply to your local context. If you are a pastor currently assigned to a church, I would like to encourage you, whether or not there is currently a state of conflict, to make use of a professional conflict trainer to strengthen your members and your leadership team in this vital ministry of reconciliation.

Ministerial students, take heart. Do not be afraid of the challenges before you. What you need to do now is to make it your personal business to avail yourself of all the continuing education in conflict resolution that you can get your hands on when you graduate and begin your ministry. Enter the ministry with an open mind to learn and never stop learning. Make a commitment to the Lord that you will be the best servant leader that you can be, according as how God has blessed you with spiritual gifts and the fruit of the Spirit. Embrace the reality that the church you will be assigned to is not perfect. I have given you some very raw facts and hopefully a reality check in this book. None-the-less, be strong and of a good courage, for God is with you in this great ministry to which He has called you.

To all local elders and church members who read this book: My prayer is that this work has given you an insight into church leadership from the pastor's perspective, one that has hopefully opened up your heart to be even more committed to working closely with your pastor in the work of the ministry. As you serve, with a more enlightened understanding and a heart subdued by the love of God, may your labors bear much good fruit for the kingdom, and may your fruit remain until Jesus comes with the voice of an archangel, and with the trump of God... to once and for all... deliver His Church from holy hell to hallelujah forevermore!

APPENDIX

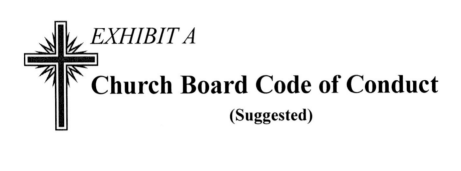

EXHIBIT A

Church Board Code of Conduct
(Suggested)

By Dr. Everton A. Ennis

1. The Board is delegated the authority to conduct the normal business of the church, reporting its activities to the full church membership at the business meetings. The Board shall have authority to appoint and recall committees and their members, and to provide for the filling of any vacancies in elected offices that may occur, by nominating a successor to the church for election (to complete the current term).

2. A quorum of five (5) members, not including the chairperson, shall be empowered to transact the business of the Board. The primary purpose of the Church Board is to plan for evangelism in all of its phases. Meetings shall be held in person (face-to-face), by telephone conference call, or via other agreed-upon media. At no time shall any member of the Board cause or allow an unauthorized person to listen in on, or to hear Board discussions via conference call (by using an extension, placing the call on speaker phone, etc.) or by making any unauthorized recordings of any meeting.

3. In event of emergencies, the Pastor is authorized to make financial decisions of up to $500.00 per month, in consultation with the finance committee (e.g., to avoid or correct emerging code violations that demand immediate attention; broken utility equipment; events hazardous to health and life; issues affecting the security, safety and proper operation of the facilities; emergencies of similar magnitude or scope). A report of the transaction shall be submitted to the Board at its next meeting by the Treasurer.

4. Discussions are conducted in an honest and mutually respectful manner. Where the personal life of individuals is concerned, confidentiality MUST be respected, and their dignity preserved at all times. No inappropriate and negative attitudes, behaviors, and words will be tolerated in the Board meetings.

5. Biblical Conflict Resolution – Being intentional about preventing avoidable inter-personal problems, and honestly and humbly dealing with those that do occur (we embrace the ethic that love does not intentionally hurt others, nor does it justifying offensive behavior or blame the hurt and offended party, thus prolonging conflict and pain).

6. Appropriate Forum – Insuring that we air personal grievances to the person concerned in private, instead of bringing them up in a public forum, unless that is where the grievance was caused; and not inciting or supporting others to violate this principle. This is considered a serious violation of this Code.

7. The Pastor serves as spokesperson for the church. All Board decisions shall be communicated by the Pastor or the Pastoral Assistant for Administration (Head Elder), unless otherwise delegated to other members of the Board. This is especially important when dealing with sensitive personal matters.

8. Confidential documents, including minutes that will be placed in your possession, are not to be duplicated or shared with unauthorized persons. The church will hear from the Pastor or Head Elder concerning actions taken. Under no circumstance should confidential Board information or documents be shared with individuals who are not members of this church, unless required to do so by order of a court and/or the South Atlantic Conference.

9. The position of servant leadership which you have accepted in the church formed the basis for your membership on this Board. Board membership is a highly responsible privilege of trust. It is a fiduciary responsibility. The Pastor and members appreciate your willingness to serve on the Board, and request that you make every reasonable effort to attend all meetings. After three consecutive unexcused absences from regular meetings, or general inconsistent attendance, the Board member may be replaced (this does not apply to called or emergency meetings). Be sure to contact the Pastor, Head Elder or Clerk if you will be unable to attend a meeting.

10. It is respectfully requested that you confer with the Pastor or your supervising Elder if you experience any difficulty in the discharge of your duties as an officer of the church or a member of this Board. It is considered courteous if you seek to resolve conflicts or difficulties before quitting your position without fair notice or without giving the leadership of the church a fair opportunity to assist you in resolving any difficulties you may have. Persistent non-attendance at church services and Board meetings, and neglect of duty shall be cause for removal from office and the Board.

EXHIBIT B

The Elders' Ten Commandments

By Dr. Everton A. Ennis

1. You shall love your fellow elders and the pastor. Honor them highly for their work's sake.

2. You shall treat fellow elders and the pastor with due respect, just like you desire to be treated with respect. Elders should be present when scheduled to serve, and shall consistently manifest the spirit of Christian cooperation and support in service alongside other elders and the pastor.

3. You shall not use the office of elder for self-glory, to gain "power" or to draw away disciples after yourself. You shall be a good example in servant leadership and Christian unity.

4. Remember to keep holy things holy. Do not use the sacred things of God for disallowed purposes. The tithe is holy unto the Lord, and elders should return the full tithe unto Him. Elders should support the local church by giving liberally to the church budget. Elders should respect the Sabbath, respect the holy services of the church, and lead their household to do likewise.

5. Honor your colleagues and the pastor, so that your working relationship with them may be well. Elders shall refrain from angry speech that diminishes others and the meetings of the church.

6. You shall not wear out your pastor by placing undue burdens and expectations on him. Help him to bear the burden of the work by teaching members to walk with God. Pastoral ministry is very complex work which no one person can effectively perform. Do not discourage the pastor by joining members in constant and negative criticism, unkind gossip, and defaming his character through slander. The elder and his family should not be guilty of such divisive and destructive behavior, but should correct, exhort and rebuke those who engage in this evil, unproductive act.

7. You shall preach the unadulterated Word of God, never your own opinion. Feed the flock over which God has made you an overseer. Minister to the people with love, understanding, grace, tact, skill, and wisdom, but also with courage and truth. Adhere to proper protocol in all things.

8. You shall not be double tongued. Do not steal or impair the good name and influence of other elders or the pastor by indulging in behind-their-back conversations with people of impure motives and unruly attitudes. The act of stealing another's good name and influence is a satanic behavior which undermines and destroys confidence in the victim's influence and leadership.

9. You shall not participate in, or allow lies, false rumors, destructive gossip, slander and evil speaking to have any place in your house or the house of the Lord. Elders should prayerfully insure that they and their own household are not guilty

of these sins which destroy the spiritual and social fabric of the church. Elders should not practice pretense, but shall speak privately, honestly and respectfully with elders or the pastor about any personal disagreement with them.

10. You shall not covet or interfere with the assignments of other elders. Do your own job well and all will be well. Do not covet the pastor's role or yield to the temptation to be the pastor's critic or supervisor. Do your own work faithfully, and so help the pastor carry the heavy load he bears.

EXHIBIT C

The Pastoral Staff

Our Purpose, Relationships & Responsibilities

By Dr. Everton A. Ennis

Our Purpose

The Pastoral Staff model of leadership was established by the Early Church, under the inspiration of the Holy Spirit, and in harmony with the wise counsel given to Moses by Jethro many years earlier. My Pastoral Staff model currently consists of the pastor and all serving elders, and exists for the purpose of providing a unified, competent and rightly motivated team of servant leaders committed to ministering to God's people, teaching them how to have a personal connection with Jesus, and inspiring them to share their love for God with others.

Our Relationships

We strive for these biblical relational ideals within the Staff:

1. Key Texts – John 13:34-35; 1 Corinthians 13; 1 John 4:7-11

2. Definition of Relationship: "A <u>connection</u> with those with whom we have to do"

3. Loving Relationships - Staff members should be kindly affectioned one to other

4. Mutual Respect - In all things and at all times, treating each other with courtesy

5. Harmonious Action - Manifest cooperation and unity to accomplish the Lord's work

6. Emotions & Manners - No inappropriate and negative attitudes, behaviors, and words

7. Truth & Honesty – Not misrepresenting others' words or impugning their motives

8. Biblical Conflict Resolution – Being intentional about preventing avoidable inter-personal problems, and honestly and humbly dealing with those that do occur (We accept that love does not intentionally hurt others, nor does it justifying offensive behavior or blame the hurt and offended party, thus prolonging conflict and pain)

9. Appropriate Forum – Insuring that we air personal grievances to the person concerned in private, instead of bringing them up in a public forum, unless that is where the grievance was caused; and not inciting or supporting others to violate this principle

Our Responsibilities

Our responsibilities to each other and the membership include:

1. Key Texts – 1 Timothy 3:1-7; 2 Timothy 3:1-4:5; Titus 1:1-3:15; John 3:16-17

2. Definition of Truth: The Word of God!

3. Care of the Church by promoting and supporting what is right, correcting the wrong

4. Uphold the distinctive Adventist message, first at home, then before the church

5. Contribute to the meeting agendas and support decisions that are properly voted

6. Faithfulness in discharging our specific assignments so the church may be edified

7. Showing respect and priority for services, meetings, ministry events, and programs

8. Make soul winning our personal priority, and inspire the membership to do the same

9. Lead with love, wisdom, tact, skill, understanding, courage, fortitude and truth

About CLASS Act Seminars

I founded CLASS Act Seminars in 2006 (registered as an LLC in 2010) as a consulting, coaching and teaching ministry to assist pastors and churches in addressing various leadership needs. A fundamental principle of CLASS Act Seminars is that no one person can effectively pastor a church! Pastors are leaders in team ministry. It is God's will for the entire body of Christ to work together to edify (build up) the body. All the spiritual gifts are needed in the process of doing the work of God. That means every member, rightly trained and motivated, and guided by insightful, faithful, visionary leaders.

It is my hope that as a pastor, you are experiencing the joy of ministry. However, if you currently find yourself in some of the darkest days of your ministry, please delay no longer to give me a call. By God's grace, wherever we have provided services to assist a pastor and his church, there has been a noticeable and refreshing turnaround in attitudes, issues and mission-mindedness... all to the honor and glory of God!

In addition to our consulting and teaching ministry in congregational conflict resolution training, CLASS Act Seminars assists pastors and churches in the development, empowerment, and training of their local leadership team, one of the crucial factors in accomplishing the church's mission. Be sure to get a FREE consultation today to see how we may be of assistance!

Website: www.classactseminars.com

CPSIA information can be obtained
at www.ICGtesting.com
Printed in the USA
FFOW03n1627090116